# NULLIFYING
# GOD

To Sprachi,
Hope you enjoy
H Robert Wilson PhD

As a publisher, I have seen many books on the subject of Creation versus Evolution and over the years have published a few. While unusual for a publisher to write an endorsement, I believe *Nullifying God* is distinctive, authoritative, and accessible, and that Dr. Wilson gets to the heart of the matter: to dismiss Creation is to dismiss God. *Nullifying God* will be a valued resource to your library.

—Dr. Samuel Lowry, Publisher

President and CEO, Ambassador International

Knowing him as a biologist, there is no doubt in my mind that Dr. Wilson knows what he is talking about. More importantly than that, however, is his unique ability to lead the reader with clarity and winsomeness into big concepts like "abiogenesis" and "homeostasis," all the while showing how a random universe is simply an impossibility. Through it all, he shows his clear love for both God and people. Dr. Wilson wakes the reader up to the beauty, intricacy, and interconnectedness of all life and Creation, and helps us stand with him in awe of the Creator.

—Brian Recker

Pastor, One Harbor Church in Beaufort, NC

I have read several books on evolution, but all were written from the reference point of Geology, Theology, and Thermodynamics. Dr. Wilson's *Nullifying God* is entirely different, because it focuses on Biology and the hard science required for life. Additionally, it provides and explains for the reader the evolutionist's main arguments and standings for their secular beliefs. I found the facts on Professor Armitage and the Triceratops (Chapter 9, "*Nullifying God*") were especially reinforcing due to his expert discussion and analysis of cell life, which was new information to me, and earth radioisotopes not being a reliable indicator of earth's true age, which reinforced information I knew about.

—Michael F. Dolan

Lieutenant Colonel, USMC (Retired)

Author Dr. Wilson is equal parts scientist and Christian, which is what sets *Nullifying God* apart from other books on the subject of evolution. He explains science to the Christian and Christianity to the scientist in making his argument that Darwin's random acts of nature cannot account for Creation.

Dr. Wilson shows that the science supporting evolution, at its core, holds biological impossibilities. Specifically, it does not and cannot answer the question, "How did we all get here?" He will tell you that he believes God is the only answer to that question. What's more is that he can tell you how he knows it to be true.

—Jane Shealy, Editor

Darwinian evolution was founded on the twin pillars of "chance" (i.e., random mutations) and "time" (i.e., billions of years). In *Nullifying God*, Dr. Wilson methodically undermines those foundations with compelling evidence of intelligent design (the fine-tuning of life) and the implications of preserved protein in ancient fossils. A fascinating and enlightening read for layman and academician alike.

—Robert Kornegay

Director, Ratio Christi at East Carolina

In *Nullifying God*, career scientist Dr. Wilson calmly points out that evolution's acceptance of evolutionary theory is based entirely on an incomplete and inadequate examination of observed evidence according to the standards of science. This lack is not only difficult for me to understand, but it directly violates the level of integrity I gained as one who entered the military service straight from high school and who retired from it at the highest Pentagon levels.

My life experiences throughout my 33 years of service were completely consistent in one respect—our Allies, other U.S. Services, Congress and our contractors always demanded precision from us with documented facts, exacting details, and proven data. It has always astounded me that those who stand on the sands of evolution will question my Christian faith by demanding rigorous, documented facts about it, yet they themselves do not provide this same stringent level of evidence for defending their position. In challenging evolution through *Nullifying God*, Dr. Wilson does exactly that by providing compelling, cogent and calm arguments for all to seriously reflect on our own beginning.

—Captain David W. Tomlinson, US Navy (Retired)


As a Christian for many years, I slowly became convinced that evolution could not explain the true origin of the species—only Creation as depicted in the Bible could do that. I was not a scientist though, and when confronted with science-trained individuals who are Christians, but also believed in evolution as settled science, I had no argument for them other than the fact that I just felt it was wrong.

Dr. Wilson's reasoned and detailed approach to highlighting the false truths of evolution in *Nullifying God* provide the lay person with the facts they need to be able to discuss the subject with science-trained individuals and refute their superiority of evolutionary knowledge.

May God use this book to spread His truth.

—Richard Truax, MBA

MAJ (retired) US Army, Retired Medical
Practice Administrator

*Soli Deo Gloria*

# NULLIFYING GOD

## Evolution's End Game

## A SCIENTIST'S
## CHALLENGE

H. Robert Wilson, Ph.D.

AMBASSADOR INTERNATIONAL
GREENVILLE, SOUTH CAROLINA & BELFAST, NORTHERN IRELAND

www.ambassador-international.com

# Nullifying God

## Evolution's End Game

A Scientist's Challenge
© 2017 by H. Robert Wilson, Ph.D.
All rights reserved

Cover Design & Typesetting by Hannah Nichols
Ebook Conversion by Anna Riebe Raats

AMBASSADOR INTERNATIONAL
Emerald House
411 University Ridge, Suite B14
Greenville, SC 29601, USA
www.ambassador-international.com

AMBASSADOR BOOKS
The Mount
2 Woodstock Link
Belfast, BT6 8DD, Northern Ireland, UK
www.ambassadormedia.co.uk

The colophon is a trademark of Ambassador

# DEDICATION

*Nullifying God: Evolution's End Game* is dedicated to my mentor, Dr. Leslie A. Stauber (1907–1973). This wonderful man was Chairman of the Department of Zoology at Rutgers University during my graduate studies. He was a true professor who taught in the laboratory as well as in the classroom by constantly challenging his students' assumptions. In the laboratory especially, he would ask *why* we were doing even the simplest task in a particular manner to ensure that we understood the implications and consequences of every procedure. Thus, he held all of his students to the highest standards of scientific inquiry. We were taught to think things through thoroughly, to never accept experimental results at their initial face value, and to always question. It was this intensive training that made my challenging the foundations of evolution possible.

# ACKNOWLEDGMENTS

The number of people who helped make this book possible is extensive, and I acknowledge each and every one of them. If I have missed any, I ask those individuals to please forgive me. I especially want to thank my wife, Lynn, for her constant encouragement and support. Special thanks go to Charlton Burns, Kurt Carpenter, Mike Dolan (Lt Col, USMC Ret.), and David Tomlinson (CAPT, USN, Ret.) for their prayers, encouragement, and review of early manuscript drafts, and to my editor, Jane Shealy, who helped me see the "chaff" I needed to separate from the grain. My prayer warriors include many at One Harbor Church, Beaufort, NC, and women at the Coastal Carolina Center for Women's Ministry, Newport, NC. Pastor Kevin Clubb, Cape Carteret Baptist Church, Cape Carteret, NC, Rev. Curtis O. Donald, Sr., Mt. Zion Missionary Baptist Church, Beaufort, NC, and Rev. Dave Linka, All Saints Anglican Church, Newport, NC also greatly encouraged me by their personal interest in this work. Special credit belongs to Susan Howes and author Juana Mikels for leading me to my partner publisher, Ambassador International.

Two individuals especially deserve to be recognized separately: Dr. Stephen C. Meyer and the late Dr. Danny Lotz. It was Dr. Meyer's insights that evolution could not explain how required new genetic information could ever come to be that led to the writing of this book. Dr. Lotz was my first Bible study leader, and his joy and insights "opened the Scriptures" to me, to grow in knowing them and allowing me to apply them today as I have in *Nullifying God*.

Most importantly, I want to thank and gratefully acknowledge my God for inspiring and guiding me in this project. *Soli Deo Gloria!*

# CONTENTS

*"In the beginning, God created..."*

—Genesis 1:1

# CHAPTER 1

# INTRODUCTION

Some readers might think it somewhat unusual that a research scientist, especially a biologist, would write a book challenging evolution. After all, we are the ones who are supposed to be among the truest of the true believers. But that is, in fact, exactly what I have done. That said, the journey leading to this point has in itself been an incredible, God-directed challenge: first, researching, scrutinizing, analyzing, and developing all the information I have found. Then, combining that with the incredible insights He has continually given me into something that makes sense, something that clearly shows evolution is not, and can never be, what it claims to be.

Before we go further, let me assure you that I am in fact a scientist through and through. I spent my career on the "front lines" as an applied or "bench" research scientist in the laboratory. I was never an academic, or a scientist advancing new theories. I was trained in biology with a PhD degree in Zoology (**parasitology**, anatomy and **physiology**), which I followed with a Post-Doctoral Fellowship in Pathology. I had an active research career spanning three decades, much of that time in the pharmaceutical industry involved in the exciting task of finding, evaluating, and testing possible new medications against certain infectious diseases and cancer, which my colleagues and I hoped might ultimately benefit patients.

I loved what I did. I loved the process of designing experiments, analyzing their data, and then doing more experiments based on those findings. I was constantly asking questions to find out what was real for any given situation and, consistent with the way science is performed, was constantly challenged by my colleagues to defend my findings, as I challenged theirs. So, I am a scientist by training and research experience, and yet today, I *absolutely* reject evolution. But, it wasn't always that way.

## WHY I WROTE *NULLIFYING GOD*

In 1974, I became a Christian, and my life has never been the same. As 19th century evangelist Oswald Chambers pointed out so clearly, I have given up my right to myself to Him, so that I belong to Him alone. In doing so the apostle Paul could claim, "It is no longer I who live, but Christ who lives in me" (Gal. 2:20, ESV). Let there be no doubt who is my Lord and Master. But, even after my conversion, as throughout all my science career, I still accepted evolution as real because I educationally grew up with it, just accepting it, and never critically questioning whether it actually was real or not. It somehow just *was*, and as to what Scripture revealed? I believed God *created*, surely, but—I did not even attempt to reconcile Scripture's truth with the science I knew at that time. God forgive me.

So, I viewed evolution as true, until . . . About eight years ago I read a single sentence in Lee Strobel's wonderful book, *The Case for a Creator.* That sentence came from an interview with Dr. Stephen C. Meyer, who earned his PhD at Cambridge in the Philosophy of Science. Dr. Meyer has developed excellent and forceful arguments for our purposeful creation through his explanation of how all life shows the "Intelligent Design" of a Creator. In his interview, Dr. Meyer was talking about a phenomenon called the "Cambrian Explosion," in which untold numbers of new life forms—literally every group of biological organisms known today—appeared in a relatively "short" speculated time interval of around 50 million years (the Cambrian era), according to geologists' time scale.

What Dr. Meyer said that so immediately arrested my attention was:

> "The big issue is, where did the information come from to build all these new proteins, cells, and body parts?"

What I instantly realized was that he was talking about was *new* genetic information. What I "heard" Dr. Meyer say was, "where did *all* the *new* genetic information come from to build all these *new* proteins, *new* cells and *new* body parts," and by extension, *new animals*? If no new genetic information, then *none* of the rest would ever come to be. And if that were the case, then *no new animals*, and—*no evolution*!

That one stunning statement, focusing on an area of biology I knew well, instantly changed my thinking, and I knew that evolution occurring through any random, purposeless, undirected, natural process such as Darwinism requires was simply not possible biologically. If it were to have happened, it would have had to have involved *massive*, integrated, nearly simultaneous positive—not negative—*random* changes of DNA to provide the new information required for all the new organisms that came to be in the "Cambrian Explosion." That is *not* what happens when DNA divides.

Briefly, when any cell divides into two, the process of its division is under exquisite scrutiny from exacting, precise cell mechanisms, so that DNA (as well as *every* component in the cell) divides correctly and makes *identical* genetic copies of itself to preserve the information it contains (a process resulting in genomic stability). Otherwise, any changes that occur in the DNA molecule could cause diseases (such as cancer).

Can mistakes (**mutations**) happen during DNA division? Absolutely, and if they do, the cell either corrects them, initiates a "doomsday" type cycle and commits "suicide" if it can't fix them (a process called apoptosis), or the mutation could linger, in which case, the cell might be unaffected, produce disease, or die from the mutation. And note, the *only* cell type in which this could occur above bacteria and be passed on is in reproductive cells—sperms and eggs. Technically, such mutations are known as germ line (reproductive cell) mutations.

Further, any *significant positive* change—those that could alter some essential characteristic of an organism to cause it to evolve—would have to take effect *without* disrupting the organism's life processes (its

**homeostasis,** its required, constant internal environment of integrated life processes); otherwise, it would no longer live. And with *random*, uncontrolled, *massive* genetic changes that would be needed for evolution? The whole organism would die.

So, as far as evolution was supposed to have occurred in the Cambrian Explosion was concerned? It simply was not possible. It was also immediately obvious to me that those same requirements would apply to *all* new types of organisms that have *ever* come to be, not just those in the Cambrian Explosion. No, evolution could not be possible, and if it were ever to have occurred, it would have to have been minor (at best a new species). My science training took over, and I began critically questioning and researching this "science" and have been since that time.

The more I looked into what evolution taught in accepted textbooks and standard reference materials, the more I found that it was not the science, not the truth, and not the fact it claimed to be. Whatever Darwin intended or thought initially, today it is clear that evolution is actually being actively promoted by its proponents and advocates, whether intentionally or not, to reduce God to a myth, to nullify Him, to get rid of Him in our lives, in our thinking, in our classrooms, and, yes, even in our churches. In other words, at its core, evolution is attempting to make us question our identity as God's Creation, His children.

That said, I *absolutely* believe the first five words in the Bible as stated in Genesis 1:1 and so clearly affirmed throughout all of Scripture: "In the beginning, God created . . . ." Not just life and every living creature, but *every* physical and natural thing that we could ever become aware of. And especially of us, who are special to God beyond all understanding, who alone are formed in His image (Gen. 1:22), and to who alone He gave His *own* breath of life (Gen. 2:7), the life that Jesus came to restore us to in relationship to Him.

I can read about Creation; I can write about Creation, but the magnificence of what those verses reveal to me will forever be beyond my understanding. And, I am at peace with that.

## WHAT TO LOOK FOR AS YOU READ

To begin: Sometimes . . . *sometimes* before you can build a new house, you must tear the old one down to the ground. Nothing must remain, including its foundation.

So it is with evolution.

When you finish reading *Nullifying God . . .* , it is my hope that you will find that evolution has no reasonable grounds to claim, as it does, that it is truth as well as scientific fact. It is my hope that you will know that only faith-based Creation alone adequately explains the mystery of all life.

To reach that endpoint, we first will be dealing with truth, science, and fact as these are found in the natural world. Just as in any other field or endeavor, truth in science depends on two key standards for people to independently reach a conclusion: 1) that they are given accurate, complete, specific, and pertinent information, and 2) that any information is presented objectively in an as unbiased manner as possible.

Equally as important as what information you are given is what information is *not* given—that is, the information that is *omitted*, whether inadvertently or purposefully. The test for whether such omitted information should be included is that if you were to find it, it would likely change your mind in making a decision, or at least make you question it. Keep in mind that all information can be argued from a particular point of view.

One last thought: This book is written to be a basic but comprehensive introduction to critique evolution. In that manner, it is not a textbook, but a handbook to this very complex, confusing, and extensive subject. The reason? Science written for professionals in peer-reviewed journals and reference textbooks is usually in-depth, with content detailed for the particular audience of the subject; it correctly assumes that those interested have the background and training necessary to understand the significance of the material presented. The field of evolution science written for professionals is no exception.

In contrast, *Nullifying God* is written by a Christian biologist for Christians and other readers who are not familiar with science. That is, it is written in a straightforward, easy-to-read narrative manner, presenting only need-to-know information that you, the reader, can directly apply to the subject at hand to make it your own. In that way, it is designed to empower and benefit you in understanding the critical essentials of evolution and its consequences, whether you have a science background or not. It does so by: 1) guiding you into solid, clear knowledge of why evolution is biologically impossible, 2) providing you with core principles of applied science to rationally question its claims, and 3) showing you that biblical Creation is the *only* reasonable and plausible answer for life.

So, because this book is a basic introduction, the text includes only the limited amount of necessary science, biology, and other specific detail needed to help you focus on understanding the issues and not get bogged down by too much information.

Occasionally, you will find words identified with bold text. These are glossary terms, which are defined in the "Glossary" after Chapter 11.

## A GENERAL GUIDE

You will regularly find Scripture in the text, so that Truth will be your constant companion. Let me explain . . .

**Why This Book Takes a Comprehensive Approach to Evolution.** Evolution is a tightly woven fabric of confusing information and claims. Many excellent and detailed science-based challenges have been made to show that Creation is the *only* reasonable explanation for all life as we know it.

However, because evolution is a fabric, any challenge must be made to its entirety, point-by-point, in order to refute it. To keep focused on its foundations, the challenge must be made at an overview level; otherwise, we could get lost in a mountain of unneeded detail.

**What Our Approach to Evolution Will Be.** Because the field of evolution studies is presented as *evolutionary biology*, it should be correctly classified as a science. Specifically, we need to treat it as the natural science it is—biology. Because this field of science objectively determines the true facts about life in our natural world through hard evidence and reason, this book will treat evolutionary biology as the science it claims to be.

Thus, in terms of it being a science, evolution would have to have taken place without Divine Creation, because, consistent with Darwin's theory, it asserts that: 1) the *origin* and 2) the evolution (diversification) of *all* life is due to *entirely* natural, random processes. There can be only one conclusion to this approach: Evolution proclaims that *all* life occurred *independently* of God and His Creation.

That being the case, we will treat it as the approach to life it is, one that is based entirely on human reason alone. *We will apply an unflinchingly and unapologetic naturalist critique to any discussion of evolution and the evidence it provides in any of its three parts* (as would be done by an evolution advocate to Creation). This critique will be based *strictly* on the established, rigorous, and accepted standards of a natural science. All natural sciences *depend on purposefully demonstrated evidence, and that will be the standard here.*

However, I would urge individuals who reject Creation to carefully consider the conversation God had with Job in Chapters 38–41 of the Bible, and in particular, Job 38:3–4, when God confronted Job:

> *3 Brace yourself like a man;*
> *I will question you,*
> *and you shall answer me.*

> *4 "Where were you when I laid the earth's foundation?*
> *Tell me, if you understand."*

Then keep in mind Job's ultimate confession (Job 42:5-6):

> *5 "My ears had heard of you*
> *but now my eyes have seen you.*

*⁶ Therefore I despise myself*
*and repent in dust and ashes."*

**Information You Will Find in Your Journey.** This book contains four general types of information:

1)  that which you need to build the foundation to apply to and understand evolution and its many problems

2)  what evolution *actually* claims and says about itself

3)  the real-world limitations of those claims

4)  the straightforward refuting of many of those claims

From this information, you will be able to clearly see, point-by-point, the outright (and likely unintentional) deception that evolution is in presenting itself as accepted fact. You will also understand how its staunch advocates and activists—although certainly not all of evolution supporters—are using evolution to attempt to nullify God in our lives.

# CHAPTER 2

# DEFINITIONS

*"If you know the enemy and know yourself, you need not fear the result of a hundred battles. If you know yourself but not the enemy, for every victory gained you will also suffer a defeat. If you know neither the enemy nor yourself, you will succumb in every battle."*

Sun Tzu (544–496 BC), *The Art of War*

In looking at the title you just read—Definitions—you're probably wondering, "An *entire* chapter set aside for definitions? What in the world?" Well, I wouldn't blame you if you were to ask that. The answer is that this information is vitally important as a foundation for understanding and critiquing evolution. We need clear definitions not only to give us the solid foundation to understand the discussions to come but also to ensure that we can critique evolution as objectively as possible.

## WHY DEFINITIONS?

To begin: When it comes to truth, remember that Jesus Christ is *the* standard, the *true and absolute* standard (Jn. 14:6). Everything involving truth as applied to any of our thinking, event, or situation about life should attempt to conform to that level of clarity. So, as in faith, it should be in science, a *human* effort, a tool, developed and used to define and characterize what is real and true in the natural world. To do this, science requires clear definitions in every respect of its use, not only because they promote understanding and communication but also because *they set standards* by which to compare and judge any work of science. Without clear, concise standards, all else falls apart in science.

To achieve this, it is the individual's striving for that level of truth that is key, despite the human failings and biases that we all have. Those who work with science are especially constrained to report their findings accurately and completely, to the best of their ability, and—*that* reporting *must* be done with words. So, if science does not properly define and use words to set rigorous standards, not only can words be used to mislead and manipulate, but they can also muddle and gloss over important distinctions needed to make some concept clear and unambiguous. Evolution is not exempt, because it asserts the certainty of being true as would any natural science, as you read earlier.

The role of the scientist in all of this is beautifully explained by Dr. Cory Franklin, the former director of a medical intensive care unit for over 20 years, and one who is well versed in science:

> "Science is about explaining nature. The scientist's role is not to tell the public what to believe. It is to clarify ideas, as efficiently as possible, so the public can understand the questions at hand."

Dr. Franklin's position does not appear to be the case with those who hold that evolution is true. Were you to study reference and text-book evolution literature, you would find that those sources define most terms in an ambiguous and broad manner that can be used at any time to favor their positions, which then becomes an "anything-the-way-you-want-it" approach. It allows evolution to change the clear meaning of terms, set its own standards, and control the narrative. Such an approach would fit well with the current philosophical movement of "postmodernism." In postmodernism, there are no absolute standards; everything becomes relative to one's point of view. Science is not exempt from this drift but can become what is known as post-normal science, where science is subordinated to cultural whims (see Appendix I).

This chapter looks at four basic but important terms:

- science
- random
- fact
- evolution

All are regularly used throughout the remaining chapters. Science, random, and fact come into play because evolutionary biology directly applies them in such a manner to justify that what it says is true. To make certain there is no misunderstanding, all terms will be defined specifically as they would be used in any good science laboratory. In that manner, they will be applied directly and in the proper context to evolution.

Evolution uses the first two terms, *science* and *random events*, to support its assertion that it is a true and valid explanation of how life originated and progressed due solely to natural events. Then, the third term, *fact*, the favored term evolutionary biology uses to assert itself to be true, will be presented in the same manner.

Lastly, *evolution* will be defined as it applies to the field of evolution science and in the strictest sense possible. This step is necessary because evolution biology presents evolution as a forgone conclusion, allowing no skepticism as required by science. For example, consider this definition of life by the National Aeronautics and Space Administration. It does not allow any consideration that evolution might not be fact, but rather restricts the explanation for all life to evolution in that it is "a self-sustaining chemical reaction capable of *Darwinian evolution*."

## SCIENCE: WHAT IT IS, WHAT IT IS NOT

Evolutionary biology supporters assert that evolution is a "science;" for example, evolution proponent Bill Nye says that "evolution came to us by . . . scientific discovery," and "naysayers [of evolution cast] doubt on science," and then from the popular media, "the science of evolution."

That being the case, we need to briefly talk about science as "science"—not how it's applied, but what it is in principle, how it's done, and what it is not. We must take this approach if we are going to effectively judge evolution by the science it claims to be. We do this in two steps: "What Science Is," and "What Science Is Not."

**What Science Is.** One of the core tenets basic to the scientific method is that those who propose a theory (in this case, evolution supporters) have the *total* responsibility of defending it, similar to a prosecutor's burden of proof in a court of law. Anyone, at any time, can challenge a theory or question the theory, *providing* that the question is rational and relevant. The questioner does not even have to be a trained scientist, because any individual can observe, think, reason, and work to a correct conclusion, providing the evidence he or she is working with is sufficiently complete. That individual can also identify gaps or missing pieces to the particular science puzzle they are thinking about.

Anyone who is actively involved in doing science, whether it be in clinical medicine, in the laboratory at the bench, in the field, or in an administrative capacity monitoring and evaluating clinical trials of new drugs—it makes no difference—any such individual *must* maintain an ever constant awareness of what science is and what it is not. Blogger Pierre Gosselin, a mechanical engineer and amateur meteorologist living in Germany, expresses the need for such vigilance perfectly:

> "Science does not progress by insisting you have the right answer from the outset. . . . Science has nothing to do with excluding, altering, and filtering data you don't agree with. And it certainly has nothing to do with shutting down open debate and the expression of alternative ideas."

Even though science is supposed to be "pure," decided only on the most objective and confirmed evidence and free from bias, it obviously at times is not. The reason? Science is a product of human effort, human reasoning, not of some outside absolute standard. Thus, science, as wonderful and practiced to the highest standards as it may be, is *never* perfect, complete, and free from error. Human personalities, faults, and frailties affect it, just as they do any other human activity.

That said, most scientists I have known and worked with over the years were highly principled and as honest, stringent, and rigorous in doing and presenting their effort as you could imagine. They constantly strove to assure that the experiments they performed and data their laboratories produced were, in fact, as of high quality as they could have been. When errors or weaknesses were found in their work during informal or formal critiquing, they accepted comments and suggestions positively to make their work better in the future.

However, because scientists are human just like the rest of us, problems can occur when egos and personalities become involved, as they inevitably do.

First and foremost, when you read anything about science, always keep clear that there is a distinction between what science *can do* or *how it is used* and, at its core, *what it actually is*.

So, what is science, then? At its core, it is no more than a tool, a tool that can sometimes be incredibly detailed and elegant in its methods and findings and the way it is used. But, at the end of the day, it is *only* a tool. Beyond that, it is a tool developed by human reasoning and experience, and therefore subject to all the biases we humans have. Therefore, it is not, and can never be, perfect.

But at the same time, it is a phenomenal tool to explore and study what is real about the natural world, and it is the only one we have to do that. To fulfill that responsibility, science has set up tested standards to minimize the chances of making mistakes and reaching false conclusions. So, *no one can make of science whatever they might want it to be.* In other words, someone working in science is essentially prohibited from molding it to meet their particular standards. Rather, *they are required to meet science's standards.*

Thus, the purpose of any science that studies the natural world for what it is (i.e., a natural science such as biology, chemistry, physics—and evolutionary biology) is to determine what is real, true, and factual about it. Further, any natural science is ruled by sets of laws that *predict* processes and behaviors of anything that exists in nature, all of which—within our ability to understand them—are orderly.

And yes, always keep in mind that because evolutionary biology is considered a branch of biology, and because it attempts to explain something about the natural world, it is clearly a natural science from beginning to end.

Today, however, the term *science* sometimes seems to be used very loosely in ways that don't appear to have any connection to the exacting, purposeful, disciplined tool you just read about. For example, think of how many times you regularly hear the words *science* or *scientist* as presented in the news or popular media. Science is referred to in just about every conceivable usage, some of which are truly trivial, such as:

- "Discovery Clarifies Soda-pop *Science . . .*"
- "'Science of Beer' goes on tap . . ."

The word *science* used in this manner may not have been applied improperly, but it makes the work sound so official, so formal, and so . . . authoritative. What it implies, however, is most definitely *not* trivial. That is, that any findings reported must be real and true, just because "science" was somehow involved. And to be fair, maybe that's the case and maybe it's not, but the bottom line is that simply *using* the word *science* doesn't make what was done "science."

Moreover, and more importantly, such apparently trivial use of the word *science* glosses over a key issue of science: As good as any results obtained might have been for the project at hand, those of us who have worked with science in an applied laboratory environment know that there is always more to be learned. Specifically, we know from experience that the whole, complete answer that takes in and tests every conceivable piece of information from the natural world is beyond our grasp. There is always one more thing we do not know. Consider Albert Einstein (1879–1955). This distinguished man can be thought of universally as the scientist's scientist, but even for a school child, his name and science are practically synonymous. What did he have to say about the lack of absoluteness in science? In this simple but elegant statement, he demonstrates this foundational element of science as well as his humility and wisdom:

"No amount of experimentation can ever prove me right; a single experiment can prove me wrong."

"A *single* experiment can prove me wrong." One *single* experiment . . . think about it. That fact highlights a core principle of science, the need for scientists to *always be skeptical* about their own or other scientists' work, always seeking to confirm or find flaws in it. Moreover, that knowledge should forever humble anyone who is active in science from making absolute statements in any capacity.

For science to achieve its goal of finding what is true in the natural world, any conclusions it reaches must be based on factual, confirmed evidence *obtained from direct demonstration made through purposeful observational studies or specifically designed experiments.* In either case, the outcome of either approach is *not* known ahead of time (although it may be hoped for); it can only be predicted. Otherwise, there is no purpose in doing the study, because you already know the answer. The goal of either type of study is to develop evidence that might be best described as **"direct evidence"**—evidence that is so clear, so tangible, so convincing that it "does *not* require any reasoning" process (i.e., **inference**) to draw a valid conclusion, although it may certainly need further work to confirm its findings.

So, how important is purposeful demonstration to finding the truth in nature? Among many others, we have to go back some years to the Greek philosopher and scientist Aristotle (384–322 BC). He is reported as having defined science as *"sure* and *evident* knowledge obtained from demonstrations [in today's terms, 'experiments']."

More recently, Nobel-prize-winning theoretical physicist Dr. Richard Feynman (1918–1988) reaffirmed this requirement for purposeful experiment or observational study in a 1964 lecture. He began by stating three core principles needed in the process of determining whether a piece of science might be true or not.

- First, from an observation we have made, we try to figure out what its scientific principle might be or how it might work.

- Second, if what we have guessed were correct, what consequences might we look for that we can test?

- Third, we *compare* our guess *directly* to what actually happens in nature through "experiment or experience" to see how accurate our guess is in predicting the outcome.

He then states the critical point inherent in science: that if our guess disagrees with experimental results, then *what we have guessed is wrong*. He sums up his discussion by saying (my emphasis):

> "In that simple statement is the key to science. *It does not make any difference how beautiful your guess is, it does not make any difference how smart you are, who made the guess, or what his name is—if it disagrees with experiment, it is wrong.*"

Notice Dr. Feynman states the requirement for "experiment" as an axiom, something that is self-evident and true when he says, "If it doesn't agree with experiment, *it is wrong.*" Keep this *absolute* need for demonstration—designed experiment or purposeful observational study (such as those involved in establishing the truth of Intelligent Design)—clearly in mind when we talk about evolutionary biology and then consider whether evolution is what it asserts itself to be or not.

One point about experiments and never having an absolute final answer before we move on: *every* experiment, *every* conclusion has limitations, and therefore, for any study, any theory, any conclusion, the specific limitations of each *must* be stated so there are no misunderstandings. We will talk about these next.

And then, the final and perhaps most important point: All science is based on the scientific method that sets the standards for how science is carried out. The need for set, exacting standards is nothing new. How important are they? Hear what Galileo (1564–1642) said so elegantly but truthfully, then keep the need for rigorous standards in mind when we discuss the field of evolution (my emphasis):

"By *denying* scientific principles, one may maintain any paradox."

In other words, without such standards, anyone can make of science whatever they want.

One central point of the scientific method that applies to *any* science study—and especially to our challenge to evolution—is this: Those asserting that what they have studied is true, that it is fact, *must* prove their case with evidence—clear, convincing, complete, direct evidence as we just talked about. In other words, the "burden of proof" is *entirely* on the ones holding to a theory, *not* the ones challenging it.

Not only that, but *any* aspect of a science study or theory is open to close and rigorous questioning that the supporter is *required* to answer, even with an "I don't know," or a "Good question, but we haven't studied that yet." Such questions especially would address the study's:

- design and methodology
- data and their analyses
- results and their interpretation
- conclusions
- any further theories arising from those studies

In short, those who challenge any aspect of science have every right to do so, just as we have the right to challenge evolution as truth. However, they should do so as knowledgably as they can to make their questions pertinent and effective, and of course, they must ask with respect.

On the other hand, we who affirm Creation as truth have *no* obligation to prove our case. That said, we must always be ready to present it as best we can with the hope that we might introduce someone to our Savior, Jesus Christ. In this, keep Peter's admonition clearly in mind:

"Always be prepared to give an answer to everyone who asks
you to give the reason for the hope that you have. But do this
with gentleness and respect . . . " (1 Pt. 3:15).

**What Science Is Not.** Now that we know some basic principles
of applied science, we need to briefly talk about "What Science Is Not."
We need to do this not only because certain aspects of how evolution
are presented clearly fall woefully short of science standards, but more
especially, because evolution *claims* to *be* science. Not only science, but
also because it dogmatically claims to be "fact" with an absoluteness
that rules out being questioned or disputed. Three points in particular
apply to evolution:

- limitations inherent in study or theory must be identified
  and stated
- deceptive reasoning techniques
- pseudoscience characteristics

**1. Limitations Inherent in a Study Must Be Identified and Stated.**
To get a good feel for how important it is for scientists to clearly state
the limitations of their study and its conclusions, let's identify how Dr.
Feynman emphasized this point as a standard for graduating science
students in a commencement address at Caltech in 1974 (my emphasis):

- "you should report *everything* you think might make [your experi-
  ment] invalid . . . "
- "details that could throw doubt on your interpretation *must be
  given,* if you know them . . . "

Notice Dr. Feynman's emphasis: "report *everything*" in terms of
your experiment(s) possibly being invalid, "*details* that could throw
doubt," and then he drives the point home with this phrase, "*must* be
given." *Full disclosure and transparency of a scientist's work is mandated.*
No "wiggle room" or fudging is allowed. That approach is required
of anyone who works in science, and it is inherent in the scientific
method. Even though there will always be some bias (keeping in mind
that scientists are human), investigators must do their best to present

an accurate, objective picture of the work they have done to the best of their ability; otherwise, what's the point?

Dr. Feynman is not alone in emphasizing this requirement. Up until 2015, a national premier medical journal, the *Annals of Internal Medicine*, required authors submitting a clinical study for publication to "Discuss the *limitations* of the present study and any methods used to minimize or compensate for those limitations." The bottom line: Discussing limitations of any science study is a universal requirement of science.

However, if someone wants to speculate or propose possible answers to any natural event for which they do not have solid evidence or are puzzled by, they are of course certainly encouraged to do so. Future studies might provide the answer they're looking for. But—to state something in *absolute* terms, especially something that does not have critical direct evidence to support and validate it is not science. Even English biologist Thomas Huxley (1825–1895; "Darwin's Bulldog") would appear to reject absolute statements in science, when he is quoted as saying,

> "The evidence . . . however properly reached, may always be more or less wrong, the best information being never complete, and the best reasoning being liable to fallacy."

In terms of stating limitations, then: Because no science study, no set of data, no theory or field can answer *every* question, *every* one has its limitations. These should be stated clearly, without bias, and in the context of the work involved. To do so bypasses the scientific method, and the work becomes suspect at the least. There are *no* exceptions.

Not explicitly stating a study's or theory's limitations is *not* science. The field of evolution is not exempt from this standard.

But, what happens if limitations are not stated? If they are not, keep clearly in mind that scientists are like the rest of us—they are human, with all the shortcomings and biases that the rest of us have. Therefore, it could be extremely easy for them to latch on to a theory, hold it dear and defend it, regardless of whether it is true. The danger? If that were ever to occur, they have to make certain that in doing so they never fit available facts to their favorite theory rather than the other way around. Especially, they should never consider *only* those facts that are consistent with it—*every* applicable fact, consistent or not, must be considered.

**2. Logical Fallacies (Deceptive Reasoning Techniques).** In recent years, you may have noticed certain statements attributed to some science field that sound—when you think about them in terms of common sense—not quite right, or in fact downright wrong. For example, "the science is settled," or "a consensus of scientists says" (i.e., a "scientific consensus") as though someone were telling us (who might not be up to speed on the particular issue) that we have neither the experience nor knowledge to effectively question any of their conclusions. If you have, you have experienced someone who is using a deceptive reasoning technique to change your opinion to theirs.

Deceptive reasoning techniques are more properly known as logical fallacies. At least six have been used to support evolution. However, all such techniques have three features in common:

- First, they are *deceptive*, because they do not deal with what is demonstrable, true, and real. As a result they typically mislead to a wrong conclusion, whether inadvertently or purposefully.
- Second, they *appear* to be reasonable—logical—but are *not*. Rather, the argument they present is invalid from the start.
- Finally, because the argument is invalid from the beginning, "Its conclusion will be unreliable *at best* . . . [and] downright *false* at worst."

Three logical fallacies in particular are used by evolution proponents to make an assertion sound true when it cannot be supported with appropriate direct evidence:

- consensus
- appeal to authority
- the *ad hominem*

In general, if you ever hear any of these applied to *any* argument involving science—not just evolution—you should be very cautious in immediately accepting what is said as true.

***Fallacy 1: Consensus.*** When someone tells you that a scientific consensus has found any particular issue to be true, be clear that that position is opinion and *only* opinion based on limited, incomplete and indirect evidence. Some hold a scientific consensus to be one step short of an accepted theory in its level of truth, and in fact, it may be. But, should consensus' *conclusions* be given the same weight as those made from direct data? The short answer is *no*.

Consensus' major flaw in asserting conclusions to be scientifically valid is that it allows opinion, *not* direct evidence, to become "truth," as though science were a democracy. In point of fact, without solid, confirmed, experimental, or observational study data—the equivalent of direct evidence—consensus at best can only say that "we *think* this is the case but don't have the key evidence to demonstrate it."

Further, when consensus is used to support a controversial, supposedly science-based position (e.g., evolution) as "true," it is likely to be nothing more than intellectual agreement among supporters being passed off as truth; that is, it has the potential to become a form of "group think." Treat it very skeptically, never forgetting that something is likely to be drastically missing, *until* consensus' conclusion has been *documented* with experimental data as true. Without such direct evidence, scientific consensus might actually become "anti-science." Worse, it permits the vague body of "consensus" scientists to potentially be treated as an authority, an authority with whom you should not disagree, because you don't know as much as they do (see "Appeal to Authority," on the next page).

To wrap up how consensus—particularly "scientific consensus"—and its implied authority should be viewed in terms of science, first consider this wonderful insight that 19th century Russian novelist Leo Tolstoy (*War and Peace*) said about it:

"Wrong does not cease to be wrong because the majority share in it."

And then consider what Galileo so eloquently pointed out:

"In questions of science, the authority of a thousand is not worth the humble reasoning of a single individual."

***Fallacy 2: Appeal to Authority:*** This logical fallacy occurs when some authority is cited to "prove" a point rather than relying on appropriate evidence. For example, the *American Association for the Advancement of Science* (the AAAS), considered "the world's largest scientific society," asserts this position on evolution:

"Evolution is one of the most robust and widely accepted principles of modern science . . . "

The key phrase of this statement showing an appeal to authority is "the most *robust* and *widely accepted*." Were this statement to be made to us, its unstated implication would be: if "the world's largest scientific society" accepts evolution as true, then who are we to dispute it? They have said it, we should accept it, and that's that, so let's move on! This, despite common sense, good science, and Scripture to the contrary. Further, the phrase "widely accepted" again brings in the issue of an unnamed consensus accepting evolution as true.

Such statements do not detail the specific, challengeable, definitive evidence required by the scientific method. *They are assertions and opinion only.* They are simply not acceptable to draw solid conclusions from.

Finally, the AAAS leaves no doubt that evolution is not only science, but "*modern science.*" Such a description implies that evolution is *required* to adhere to all standards of a natural science.

And as far as science exerting itself as "authority?" Consider what one of our Founding Fathers, Benjamin Franklin, had to say about authority; note his use of the word *first*:

"It is the *first* responsibility of every citizen to question authority."

The bottom line: Science is not only not an authority that cannot be challenged, but anyone in science should always have some level of skepticism about anything science claims to be true.

**Fallacy 3: The Ad Hominem.** Finally, we need to look at the *ad hominem*, which plays a pivotal role in how evolution is being presented to the public as truth and fact. Simply put, an *ad hominem* (Latin for "to the man") is abusive name calling with the intent to intimidate or just plain bully a debate opponent into silence and eliminate any further discussion. In terms of evolution, for example, it occurs when someone who proclaims Creation is called an "evolution denier." This reprehensible term evokes the holocaust denier, a person who rejects a true historical event. Evolution denier originated with the *ad hominem* "global warming denier" introduced into the news media in 2007, and today called "climate change denier."

The original quote that popularized the *ad hominem* "denier" is this one by Ellen Goodman of the *Boston Globe* (my emphasis):

> "I would like to say we're at a point where global warming is impossible to deny. Let's just say that *global warming deniers are now on a par with Holocaust deniers,* though one denies the past and the other denies the present and future."

**3. Pseudoscience**. The last point we will look at in "What Science Is Not" is the issue of pseudoscience. At the practical, everyday level, defining the characteristics of a pseudoscience is fairly straightforward. The essence of pseudoscience is found in any endeavor that:

- attempts to present itself as science, *but*
- does *not* adhere to the rigorous standards of the scientific method in how it is performed, *or*
- simply *can not* be performed by the scientific method; specifically, that it . . .
- proposes hypotheses that *can not* be shown to be wrong through data obtained by direct, definitive experiment or purposeful, designed observational studies, *and*

- uses euphemisms, vague or ambiguous phrasing, and wording that can mean whatever the individual wants it to mean, and *finally*
- presents detailed evidence only consistent with its conclusions but that utterly fails to *carefully* explore (omits) evidence that is *not* consistent with them

Although evolution calls science-based Creation arguments such as Intelligent Design and Irreducible Complexity "pseudoscience" (they are not) the manner in which evolution attempts to validate itself is ironically consistent with the characteristics of a pseudoscience in many of these points. The final criterion is critical, as the following online commenter makes clear in this summary statement (my emphasis):

> "But, finding evidence consistent with an hypothesis, and failing to look for evidence *inconsistent* with it [such as is found in Intelligent Design and Irreducible Complexity studies], has ever been the foundation of pseudoscience."

Now that we have a basic understanding of what science is and is not, we need to define *random* and then *fact*.

## RANDOM

Evolution purposefully excludes God as Creator of all the life we know (and all else as well), and in doing so, it has judged itself to be nothing but secular in its explanations. That being the case, all of evolution theory *must be based on randomness and the random event at some level* (especially random changes to DNA from mutations), to be consistent with Darwinian thinking. It *cannot* be *purposeful* to the slightest degree, especially in how life originated from non-life or the process by which new organisms come to be. Because *random* is such a critical foundation to evolution's claims, we need to get a comprehensive feel for what *random* fully implies in terms of evolution. We will do this by first looking at several definitions, finding their common features, and then using those to characterize what *random* implies in terms of evolution.

*Merriam Webster's Collegiate Dictionary* [10th ed., pg. 967; 1993*]: RANDOM: "Lacking a definite plan, purpose or pattern ... random stresses lack of definite aim, fixed goal, or regular procedure ... "

*Wikipedia*: RANDOM: "the lack of pattern or predictability in events ... [having] no order and ... not following an intelligible pattern."

The *Free Dictionary* online expands these definitions with its definition of "randomness": "1. Having *no* specific pattern, purpose, or objective ... " It then includes this excellent tidbit of information (my emphasis): "2. The quality of *lacking any predictable order or plan; 'noise.'*"

And finally, this important (but somewhat dense) piece of information. It contains one more very critical characteristic we need to include—the quality of randomness being patternless, even if events were taken to *infinity*:

> "It seems clear that most of the ways an infinite sequence [of numbers] might be produced, and hence most of the sequences [of numbers] so produced, will be random," and "random sequences are thus patternless, or disorderly."

Because evolution claims itself to be nothing else but random, these definitions show that its process must be considered, in the most complete and *absolute* sense, to be *utterly* without any:

- purpose, direction, or pattern
- predictable order (i.e., it is disorderly)
- plan, outcome, or objective
- conscious input or influence

---

* The 1993 edition of *Merriam Webster's Collegiate Dictionary* was selected purposely for defining several terms in this work. This intentional use was to preclude any definitions being influenced by shifting cultural norms that have taken place over the past 20 years, for example, post-normal science (Appendix I). Such updated definitions can contain euphemisms that distort and subvert the clear meaning of words.

In other words, and again in the context of evolution, for any life developing from non-living chemicals (abiogenesis), or any new organism arising from evolution—if it occurred randomly—the process involved had to have been not only disorderly, but the final outcome just basically "happened" without rhyme, reason, or purpose. And that hit-or-miss purposelessness, even if carried to infinity, defines how evolution explains life. How sad.

One last point—and it's not a pleasant one—to follow this secular line of thinking to its logical (but depressing) conclusion, any life—including yours and mine—produced through the random process of evolution then becomes biologically purposeless in and of itself, because evolution is random, purposeless.

How that abject thinking stands in utter, stark contrast to the purposefulness of our Creator, a loving God who created the universe and gave Himself for us through His Son, Jesus Christ, so that we could know Him and the life He has for us. Recall especially what Genesis reveals to us (my emphasis):

> "Then God said, "Let us make mankind in our image, in our likeness . . . " (Gen. 1:26), and "Then the LORD God formed a man . . . and *breathed into his nostrils the breath of life . . . "* (Gen. 2:7).

Such a contrast! Evolution would teach and have us believe that for whatever unique biological qualities we have as human beings, we are nothing special beyond that. Instead, God exposes this dogma that deceives for what it is and tells us that He lovingly created us *in His image* and breathed *His own life* into us, the life that Jesus came to restore. What God tells me is beyond overwhelming and humbling, and leaves me worshipping without words.

## FACT

Why is fact so important in discussing evolution? Evolution supporters emphatically characterize evolution as fact rather than a *possible* natural explanation for life, as required by science. For example, and as you might expect, evolutionary biology science textbooks directly state that evolution is a fact. Consider the following in *Evolution* by N. H. Barton and his colleagues (my emphasis):

*"Evolution is accepted as a fact...,"* and *"The fact of evolution ..."*

Online evolution articles are easily found that more forcibly assert the same conclusion. Witness what evolutionary biologist and atheist Richard Dawkins states:

"This [evolution] is not something you believe in or not. This is a fact. It is a fact. It's just as much as fact as that the earth goes around the Sun."

Other online commentary supports evolution in stronger and no uncertain terms. Consider this unequivocal statement by an atheist group that calls those who believe in Creation "evolution deniers" (my emphasis):

*"The fact of evolution is incontrovertible..."* [and that not accepting evolution as true and real] *"constitutes a complete failure to deal with reality."*

*Incontrovertible* is a *very* strong word. It means that some position or statement is not in the least open to question, argument, dissention or controversy. In this manner, the writer seems to be attempting to shut down any possibility of discussion or debate.

**Science and Fact.** *Fact* implies an absolute quality about something. For our purposes here, think of fact in terms that are synonymous with something that is unquestionably true (e.g., the earth revolves around the sun). In other words, a fact is something that either is or is not. It is beyond any reasonable doubt or debate, and in that sense it becomes equal to an immutable truth. In science, observation and experimentation are used to *demonstrate* that a fact is actual and is truth to the limited extent that it can.

The claim of evolution theory being so strongly asserted as "fact" (*not* simply a hypothesis, or something less certain) therefore suggests the *absolute* certainty about what it is. Thus, evolution being fact forms part of the fundamental foundation for the entire field of evolution studies—life originating and diversifying from *only* random, natural events through abiogenesis. Because of this singular importance to evolution, we need to look at *fact* very closely, to define and characterize it carefully, if we would establish a standard that excludes ambiguous definitions (my emphasis in each case).

*Merriam Webster's Collegiate Dictionary* [10th ed., pg. 416; 1993]: FACT: "The quality of being *actual* . . . a piece of information presented as having *objective reality*; in fact: in *truth*."

The *Oxford English Dictionary* (via Wikipedia): FACT: "A fact is something that has really occurred or is *actually* the case . . . Scientific facts are verified by repeatable careful observation or measurement (i.e., *by experiments or other means*)."

So, what do we take away from these two definitions? Namely, that a fact is "actual," that it is "objective reality," and that it is "truth." A definition in evolution literature comes close to, but doesn't meet, the strictness of the definitions we've just read, namely that "In science, a fact is a verified **empirical** observation . . . "

Let's stop right there for a moment. As used by evolution, empirical (pronounced: ehm PEER ih kuhl) simply refers to knowledge gained by observation and experimentation, and that is correct. However, when applied to science, evolution's definition of *fact* is neither complete nor specific enough to use in day-to-day, applied science studies in a laboratory.

First, why is evolution's definition of *fact* not complete in terms of science? Look carefully for a moment and compare it to the other two definitions of *fact* and the glossary term *empirical*. Note that a single, critical word expressly stated or implied in the other definitions is missing: *experimentation*, that is, direct demonstration.

Then, a careful reading also shows that the three critical words—
*verified, empirical, observations*—are general and ambiguous rather than
specific in *how* they are to be applied. Because of those characteristics,
this last definition could be molded to support virtually any position.
Instead, a natural science (e.g., biology, chemistry, physics) requires
crisp, clear definitions that show something either is or is not in order
to be judged as fact.

Here we have to be very picky about the actual words used. Most
especially: *How* is something to be verified? The evolution definition of
fact implies that simple observation is sufficient to establish something
as fact . . . and it *could* be—*if* a scientist were describing the external
characteristics of a physical object (e.g., the moon, an unknown but-
terfly species, and—you guessed it—a new fossil). But simple observation (as distinct from a purposeful observational *study*) alone *cannot*
be used to draw valid conclusions as to the "how" of something, the
mechanics of some biochemical or other biological process, for example. Returning to Dr. Feynman's teaching, you can "guess" (make
a hypothesis) how a specific process *might* work, but then you would
need to *demonstrate*—by experiment—that your guess was true.

Perhaps the most straightforward way to consider the absolute
quality of how a fact is established in science is to look at how direct
evidence is defined for legal purposes, that is: "evidence that is gained
by *direct demonstration*," so that 1) it is "real, tangible, or clear" and as
such, 2) it does *not* require reasoning or inference to draw a conclusion.

The key words in the definition of direct evidence require that such
evidence be gained by "direct demonstration," that it is "real, tangible
and clear," and that it "does not require inference or reasoning to draw
a conclusion." In science, such evidence can be obtained *only* by one or
more definitive *experiments*, and the result may be able to constitute
fact only after the results are expanded and confirmed. Experiment
directly demonstrates that your guess either is, in whole or in part, true
and therefore fact, or it is not. If it is wrong, it is considered "falsified."

Inference may lead you to your next experiment, but it cannot be used for a final conclusion.

Recall how well Dr. Richard Feynman's short, straightforward axiom describes the critical need for experiment (my emphasis):

> "It doesn't matter how beautiful your theory [guess] is, it doesn't matter how smart you are. If it doesn't agree with experiment, *it's wrong.*"

When we later talk about how evolution draws its conclusions and claims them to be true, to be fact, keep clearly in mind the absolute nature of what constitutes fact, how a true fact requires direct evidence gained by designed experiment or a purposeful observational study. Contrast that standard, that requirement with anything that is only *asserted* to be fact through inference. The two are as different as day—and night.

## EVOLUTION

Evolution's definition below is perhaps the most intricate information you will read in this book. However, it is here that the battle lines become clear.

So, what *is* evolution? In the most general definition of the term, Webster's notes that it is a continuing process whereby one thing is worked out to become something else. In terms of Darwinian evolution, it is "a theory that the various types of animals and plants have their origin in *pre-existing* types and that the distinguishable differences are due to modifications in successive generations."

However, evolution as currently used in evolutionary biology is defined differently by independent sources that emphasize particular aspects of their arguments when they attempt to defend it. Thus, it appears to be an ambiguous term that does not clearly characterize or define what evolution actually is (or should be) at its core. Reading various sources will convince anyone that those involved do not agree on a comprehensive but straightforward definition, if one were available.

But that finding isn't surprising because evolution proponents do not always agree on definitions, for instance, what a *species* is. A recent summary noted that over 20 definitions have been proposed. In the world of biology, a species is generally taken to refer to a specific organism that is different at its core from any other organism. Further, it either will not produce offspring if mated with another closely related organism, or any offspring will be sterile. This nearly absolute specificity of a species (in mammals) is clearly shown by cloning experiments, in which the DNA of one species is inserted into the egg of another: with one exception, they don't work.

Further, developing a clear, concise statement of how evolution actually defines itself is a frustrating journey. Based on Darwinism and fossil evidence, we might reasonably expect a comprehensive science explanation and confirming demonstration of 1) how life started, and 2) when it was once formed how more and more complex animals evolved in a progression leading to man—think for a moment of the common Darwinian illustration of apes evolving to man. We might expect that, but that is not what we find.

Instead, evolutionary biology seems to provide definitions suited to its own purposes in terms of its being science and fact, the bottom line of which is: It *is* science and fact—but, at the same time, it *isn't*. Actually, evolution seems to straddle two worlds in its claims to be science. First, it confusingly considers itself a "historical process" and a "historical science," based on "Darwinian Natural Selection," but then it also must be a *natural* science because it claims to involve "Mendelian genetics," a foundation of modern biology. To add to the confusion, recall, too, the AAAS's unequivocal statement that evolution is "modern science." All of which raises the question: Is it science or not, and if not, why not?

And as far as it being a fact is concerned: evolution claims to be fact, because it is a "so well-supported" theory, and as such, *laboratory experiments are not necessarily required*. However, note that by taking this position, evolution exempts itself from the scientific method's standards that *require* direct evidence through experiment, and in that regard, keep in mind Dr. Feynman's axiom, "If [your theory] doesn't agree with experiment, it's wrong." If no definitive experiments are offered consistent with good biological science methodology, then no definitive conclusions are possible.

Thus, in that definition evolutionary biologists are able to claim "evolution" any time they can propose or demonstrate a *genetic basis* for even a minor change in an organism, for example an insect (a blowfly) becoming resistant to an insecticide.

And, the "bad news" for those of us who assert Creation, is this: Evolution proponents can legitimately claim evolution from such examples as the blowfly according to that particular definition, *but*—and here's the key and the good news—that claim is incomplete, because their claim is true *only* in the most restricted sense possible. In other words, yes, the blowfly did *technically* 'evolve' to become resistant to the insecticide *according to that very broad and all-encompassing definition* consistent with Webster's broad definition. And, true, that part of evolution *is* science and fact, because it has been demonstrated with direct evidence. However, that is where evolution's science and fact begins and also where it ends.

Now, the good news for Creation (the bad news for evolution) is that—despite the genetic change documented in the blowfly (and similar examples)—evolution of the blowfly winds up with the *same organism*, the *same* genus, the *same* species, etc. But the broad definition we've just read leading to those observations is not the end of the argument. To further totally confuse the issue, evolution is broken down into various types, which include:

1. Coevolution: organisms or features of organisms randomly evolving together in codependent relationships; there is no evolution if they don't.
2. Convergent evolution: totally unrelated organisms independently evolving similar features (e.g., fins in a fish and a whale)

3. Chemical evolution: random chemical reactions that could have evolved complex organic compounds from simple ones

4. Microevolution: minor genetic changes resulting in new features or species of an organism

5. Macroevolution: major changes that result in totally new organisms from pre-existing ones

6. Forward evolution: evolution in response to some environmental stimulus

7. Backward evolution: evolution back to the original organism when the environmental stimulus is removed

All of this background leads to the big question: How *should* evolution be defined for it to be truly *tested* as good science and for Creation to *challenge* it as science and fact? We have to pose at least two other questions set in terms of Creation to answer that critical one:

1. Aren't we arguing *against* even the remote possibility of *major* changes, such as reptiles *randomly* evolving to mammals, which ultimately *randomly* evolve to human beings?

2. Aren't we arguing *against* randomness—*the* core principle of evolution—as an explanation for the mind-boggling purposeful diversity of the life we know that is found today as well as in fossils?

Those arguments *require* evolutionary biologists to establish a discrete, narrow definition of evolution *restricted* to how entirely new *groups* of animals with utterly new and unique biologies could come to be (e.g., again, reptiles evolving to mammals) as a result of a *random biological process*. This definition would then become the required standard to compare any claim for evolution. Because biology ultimately deals with the whole animal, evolution must be able to describe and explain the comprehensive (holistic) process for any specific incident of evolution, and each piece of that process must be explored, tested by experiment, and be shown how it integrates into the whole. It has rightly been pointed out that this holistic approach should be "the *starting point* for thinking about the evolution of [any] animal."

Think back to the blowfly, for example: if evolution in the strictest sense were actually involved, then the restricted definition of evolution would at the least require some *new* insect to emerge that had *never* been seen before. It would have to have not only a unique collection of genetic information (termed its **genome**) but also significant external changes in body shape, size, or appearance (i.e., a change in morphology), as well as changes in reproductive or feeding behaviors and physiology. Such changes in an organism's biology would require significant and substantial changes to its existing genome, if not an entirely new genome, for a new organism to come into being. These features must be included in any definition to adequately describe and explain Darwinian evolution. Currently, they are not.

Moreover, until a clear, concise definition of evolution is broadly agreed to by the scientific community, its processes cannot be tested by experiment. Keep firmly in mind that such testing is required by the scientific method to determine whether a theory might be valid ("true") as a tenet of science if the results support it. Otherwise, it is not true ("false") if they don't. Without those tests, a theory is just . . . a theory.

And why must we insist on that approach? Because the seemingly insurmountable biologically massive changes required for an entirely new animal to form involve the biology of the *whole* animal (the *holistic* approach that involves preserving homeostasis mentioned earlier). Simple, minor mutations here and there, as is the case with the blowfly's insecticide resistance, simply won't do as evidence to support that one major group could ever evolve to another.

One last point: As is common in evolutionary biology, to just say that something evolved to be the way it is as an adequate explanation is absolutely wrong. Why? Because that approach 1) *presumes* that evolution is true and is fact (it's not), and 2) *must* comprehensively and carefully explain the critical issue of how entirely new groups of animals with new physiologies maintain homeostasis during their evolution—and then evolution must *demonstrate* that assertion with multiple experiments (it doesn't!). In fact, evolution entirely ignores homeostasis in its presentation and explanation of how evolution could ever occur. When the claim for evolution as fact is used in such a casual manner, evolution simply becomes an authoritarian explanation of convenience that is designed to refute being challenged and nothing more. And, *that* is not science, and it is not right.

In the next chapters, we will look at the three integral parts that constitute evolution. We will evaluate the evidence for and against each, and then we will judge whether any might be fact according to the science standards we have reviewed:

1. Abiogenesis: the natural origin of life due to random events

2. Adaptation: how each animal has an enormous amount of pre-existing genetic information that allows it to cope with a changing environment (the basis for Darwinian "Natural Selection")

3. Evolution in the strictest sense: how entirely new animals might arise from existing ones

# CHAPTER 3

# ABIOGENESIS: EVOLUTION'S RANDOM ORIGIN OF LIFE

*"Until man duplicates a blade of grass, nature can laugh at his so-called scientific knowledge."*

Thomas Alva Edison

For evolutionary biology to provide the only reasonable science-based explanation for the incredible diversity of life we see today, it had to begin by some entirely natural and random events taking place. *All* life. *No* exceptions. God could not be involved.

However, this point comes with a very loud and clear "but . . . " attached. Because evolutionary biology classifies itself as a science, founded solely on the laws of nature (that is, a natural science), it *must* abide by one *absolute* condition, if it is to be remotely considered as fact. Life had to begin from non-life, a process termed abiogenesis (pronounced ay bigh oh JEN eh sis).

Put another way, if science *cannot* demonstrate that life developed from natural, random processes with direct evidence, then evolution *cannot* be fact. Rather, such an admission would tacitly acknowledge the absolute need for a Creator, because Creation is the *only* alternative. It's that simple. It would clearly show that evolution is only a secular explanation for life, lacking the science and biology foundation it claims.

However, in the world of evolutionary biology, this situation is unthinkable and is to be instantly rejected, even though abiogenesis directly violates a proven biological law that states life can only come from life (the Law of Biogenesis). Even so, evolution proponents dismiss Creation out of hand, never seriously giving it a second thought, except when attempting to defend their position. Some evolution advocates even reject including abiogenesis as being part of the entire process of evolution. What they essentially state is that critiquing the origin of life should be separate from and have nothing to do with evolution.

That claim misdirects and is bogus. Abiogenesis and evolution are *absolutely* linked together *because they each claim that a natural, random process is responsible for both the origin and diversity of life, a process that completely and utterly excludes God and His Creation.*

That being the case, we need to spend a little time understanding abiogenesis, because evolution *must* validate the random origin of life first for *any* other part of its theory to be taken seriously. The natural, random origin of life, then, becomes *the* centerpiece, *the* foundation that underlies the *entirety* of evolutionary biology.

Darwin apparently thought that abiogenesis would never be a major issue. Witness this insightful comment by engineer and environmental scientist, Tony Heller:

> "Charles Darwin can be forgiven for having made the mistake of believing that there was such a thing as a 'simple life form.' We now know that all life, all cells, all molecules, all atoms, and all particles are incredibly complex."

Note Heller's emphasis here: *all* life, *all* cells, *all* molecules, *all* atoms, and *all* particles . . . *everything* is complex; *nothing* created is simple and straightforward. And that hurdle is a chasm that faces evolution proponents when they attempt to show that abiogenesis could ever have occurred.

With that brief introduction, we can now consider the question: What acceptable evidence does evolution provide to establish the random origin of life as *fact*? In approaching this issue, we will consider:

- the challenge facing abiogenesis to be accepted as true
- the seven biological requirements of all life

- evolutionary biology's speculation on the natural origin of life
- the direct evidence abiogenesis offers to validate the theory of evolution

## ABIOGENESIS' CHALLENGE

The first critical challenge to evolutionary biology is that it must *demonstrate* the process of abiogenesis with direct evidence to meet scientific standards. So, what is the direct evidence needed? It is the formation of a *living* organism, a viable, whole cell that can live on its own (in biology, a free-living cell).

That evidence cannot be limited to simply demonstrating the natural formation of *bits and pieces* of a whole cell (e.g., amino acids, protein fragments and other biochemicals) because that leaves no plausible explanation of how these biological bits could randomly come together to *form* a whole cell. Anything short of that demonstration cannot be used as the direct evidence needed to establish abiogenesis as fact.

To grasp the enormity of this challenge, the first critical question is this: What are the *minimum* biological requirements of life?

**Life's Seven Biological Requirements.** Any free-living organism, whether it is a single cell (e.g., a bacterium, a protozoan) or a multi-cellular, complex organism (e.g., a human being), must meet certain biological requirements in order to survive and thrive. These requirements are the foundation of all life, including that of any proposed cell that came to be as a result of abiogenesis.

Evolutionary biology considers the most primitive cell to be the "Last Universal Common Ancestor" (the LUCA), or the "Last Universal Ancestor" (the LUA). Understand that the LUCA is strictly hypothetical; evolutionary biologists have no evidence of any sort that it ever existed. Additionally, although it may not have been the first cell, it is claimed as the ancestor of all life we know today. Evolutionary biology acknowledges that the LUCA had to have been complex, had a genetic code (implying it could duplicate itself), and had a very involved metabolism.

Whether or not the LUCA was the first cell is unimportant. The crucial point here is that whatever the first cell was, or whenever it came to be, from the *moment* it gained "life," it would have to have had *every single one* of a required set of seven life processes up and running efficiently. Not only that, but the LUCA or *any* cell that came before it would have had to be able to simultaneously *control* every one of those processes in an integrated manner from the start. It would not have survived otherwise.

So—when the random mass of chemicals somehow came together and formed the first free-living, complete cell, from the very first moment that cell would have had to:

- *Acquire energy:* take in energy (for example, heat) or energy-containing chemicals (nutrients) from the environment
- *Use energy:* release the energy from energy-containing nutrients or other sources and use it to sustain every one of its cellular processes
- *Regulate its internal environment:* regulate and keep every life process balanced and stable even when the external environment is constantly changing (the physiological principle of homeostasis)
- *Transport substances:* actively move any substance that it needs from its environment into itself (e.g., water, salt, nutrients) or out of itself (e.g., waste products) through a complex functioning, living cell membrane. Such transport would have to be *selective* to prevent unwanted materials from entering the cell (e.g., too much water or salt), or needed products from leaving the cell (e.g., critical amino acids, fats, proteins and enzymes, nucleic acid precursors)
- *Synthesize and degrade substances:* make the various biochemicals it specifically needs exactly when they are needed and in the amount they are needed (e.g., for its membranes, proteins and enzymes, and the nucleic acids RNA and DNA), then break them down when they are no longer needed
- *Excrete wastes:* selectively remove wastes and used biochemicals

- *Reproduce*: make new, duplicate copies of itself (i.e., daughter cells) at the proper time and in a controlled (not random) manner consistent with its environment

As Heller emphasized, these minimum requirements clearly show that even the simplest single cell is an incredibly complex entity, because all functions must work in a highly regulated, and interactive manner. *Take any one of these away, and the cell would instantly cease to exist or would never have formed in the first place.* This very complex framework then forms the core of a virtually insurmountable scientific challenge to evolutionary biology—to demonstrate with direct evidence that abiogenesis could occur.

In contrast, Creation is simple but at the same time a mystery. In terms of human reasoning, it actually falls in line with a well-known principle of logic, "Occam's Razor," first proposed by Franciscan Friar William of Ockham in the 14th century. In essence, Occam's Razor states that *only* when the simplest explanation is *shown* to be wrong or doesn't work should more complex ones be considered. In other words, the simplest, most direct explanation—in this case, Creation—should be the first considered as the right one to explain how life came to be. In contrast, the immense complexities of the random requirements of abiogenesis set it aside as not being a tenable explanation for life.

But why should Creation be described as simple? Scripture reveals that God created life on the fifth day simply *by His word alone* when the Bible tells us, "And God *said* . . . " (Gen 1:20, 24, 26). I believe Christian author J. B. Phillips would admonish those who might feel that God was not capable of such a feat to earnestly consider just the title alone of his classic apologetic, *Your God Is Too Small.* God is unquestionably big enough to have created life. But then, Creation is a mystery because God is a mystery, and yet, He is always present to us. Look what He lovingly tells His prophet, Jeremiah:

> "Call to me and I will answer you and tell you great and *unsearchable* things you do not know" (Jer. 33:3, my emphasis).

Evolutionary biology takes a somewhat different approach to explaining the origin of life.

**Evolutionary Biology's "Origin of Life."** How does evolutionary biology demonstrate the random origin of life? The short answer is: It doesn't, it hasn't, and it can't. Rather, *every explanation it offers is nothing more than speculation*. As eminent evolutionary biologist Dr. Ernst Mayr confesses in his book, *What Evolution Is* (2001), "the cold *fact* remains that *no one* has so far succeeded in creating life in a laboratory"(my emphasis). That critical point remains true in 2016. He also notes that no one has yet determined how DNA became the master molecule of the cell that it is, a critical feature needed to document abiogenesis. And on top of all of those problems, evolutionary scientists do not even agree on a standard theory by which the first cell came to be.

Finally, evolutionary biologists can only speculate that RNA was somehow randomly formed through "chemical evolution." This event would have allowed random protein fragments to be made, and these are speculated to eventually have caused a cell to be formed. This explanation is neither reasonable nor plausible (see Appendix II).

This failure to create a living organism in the laboratory raises an interesting question: Don't evolutionary biologists have enough information about a free-living cell to create life?**

The enormity of what is known about the biochemistry, physiology, and molecular biology of the cell is hard to grasp, but we might be able to get some feel for it. For example, if you were to search a national literature database such as the National Library of Medicine for papers published on DNA since it was first reported in 1955, you would find more than 1.403 million publications, with more than 4,400 new articles each month. That amount of information on DNA *alone* (not to mention RNA, various cell functions, enzymes, and proteins, etc.) is staggering.

---

** Asking if evolutionary biologists might have enough information to create a living cell raises a second question: How much information *is* available?

The answer is: no. Given the mind-numbing number of known and still-being-discovered cell components, including a dynamic cell membrane, multiple classes of carbohydrates, proteins and enzymes, and independently functioning RNA and DNA, *all* of which would have to work in concert together, scientists are not even close. All of these components would have to be produced and successfully integrated through entirely random processes in order to demonstrate that abiogenesis *might* have occurred.

Science—which evolution claims to be—*cannot* create life and therefore cannot possibly understand how it came to be, much less what life is in and of itself. Nobel-prize-winning physicist Dr. Richard Feynman acknowledged this absolute when he simply and clearly admitted,

"What I cannot create, I do not understand."

Yet, those who promote evolution insist they can explain its processes despite the inherent complexities and unknowns that they can neither demonstrate nor create. Biochemist and Creation author Dr. Michael Behe has termed this truth "irreducible complexity" in his apologetic work challenging evolution, *Darwin's Black Box.*

As you found earlier, any scientific study has limitations and these must be clearly stated. Although Dr. Mayr correctly notes that life has not yet been created in a laboratory, he does *not* state that it is *a* limitation, indeed a fatal flaw in the theory of evolution. He does not even mention it as possibly being one.

Instead, the reality is that because evolutionary biology *cannot* and *will not* be able to demonstrate abiogenesis, it becomes *the* critical limitation that calls the entirety of life's *natural* origin into question.

Further, it leaves those who proclaim the natural, random origin of life and its diversity as fact to fall back on the logical fallacy that "life is a fact and evolution is a fact, so abiogenesis *must* have occurred." That assertion makes no sense and is not science. If evolutionary biology is not able to demonstrate abiogenesis according to the rigorous standards of science, then it is not fact, and the door to Creation swings wide open.

Because abiogenesis has not been demonstrated with direct evidence, it is not and cannot be fact, nor even be claimed to be fact. Yet, evolutionary biology is adamant that abiogenesis occurred. How is it possible for a natural science to make such an unsupported absolute claim? Let's review what evidence the natural science of evolution offers.

**What Evidence *Does* Evolution Offer to Validate Abiogenesis?** To understand evolutionary biology's position, we need to talk a little about chemistry, specifically, "prebiotic chemistry." In brief, prebiotic chemistry proposes possible routes by which the first organic molecules required for life were formed by natural, random processes before any life ever began. These compounds include 1) amino acids for proteins, and 2) sugars and nucleic acid biochemicals for RNA and DNA.

The first and most famous of prebiotic studies were the Miller-Urey experiments, performed in 1953. These and all other such chemistry studies have been based on two assumptions:

1. the likelihood that earth's original atmosphere contained methane, ammonia, and hydrogen, and

2. that these gasses combined in an aqueous (water) environment when activated by certain types of energy (e.g., lightning, sunlight, undersea volcanic gas vents) to form the first organic compounds needed for life, like amino acids.

These experiments have in fact yielded amino acids and incomplete parts of nucleic acid molecules, some of which fall apart quickly. Further, it has been shown that amino acids can slowly join together by themselves under certain conditions to form random amino acid chains and protein fragments. These studies make up the *only* experimental evidence available to support abiogenesis. Note, however, that this evidence is all indirect and circumstantial and requires inference to conclude that the various prebiotic chemicals somehow randomly worked together to form the first cell. Further, although abiogenesis has been unsuccessfully attempted in the confined, controlled laboratory environment, the problems abiogenesis would face in the unconfined, uncontrolled natural environment would multiply without limit. (See Appendix II)

Any conclusions about the origin of life beyond these prebiotic experiments are *strictly speculations*. Specifically, these conclusions include 1) that over the course of billions of years, the amino acids and other chemicals continually produced by prebiotic chemistry reactions somehow combined, 2) that they then randomly "evolved" into more complex compounds (especially RNA), and 3) that ultimately, the first life was formed. This line of reasoning is entirely speculation simply because there is *no* direct evidence showing *how* these processes worked together to form a free-living cell, the first organism. That is a critical problem for the theory of evolution.

It is also a problem for the process of DNA, necessary for cell formation. Even with the stunning advances in the molecular studies of DNA involving dozens of scientists over the past two decades, there are still parts of DNA whose function is unknown in the simplest human engineered organism. And none of the work involved in those studies was done under the random conditions that would have been present before the first organism was formed. None. Rather, all such experimental work was performed under exacting laboratory conditions with the *intent* of creating life.

## ABIOGENESIS— THE BOTTOM LINE

Abiogenesis is the proposed process by which the first cell came to be, a process from which science excludes Creation because "it is not science." Yet science claims abiogenesis *is* a fact, despite the limitation that *no living cell* has ever been produced in laboratory experiments.

In dealing with this subject as science, you must understand that the absence of that evidence does *not* mean that abiogenesis did not or could not occur. However—and this is the key issue—*without* such specific evidence, evolutionary biology *cannot* legitimately claim that a *natural*, random origin of life ever occurred and is, in fact, "fact" as it does. That being the case, the only argument evolution scientists are left with is basically this: "Life surrounds us in incredible diversity; therefore, since it had to begin somehow, and since abiogenesis is the only reasonable science-based explanation we have available, it must be true." This conclusion would be a prime error in logic, technically known as an argument from ignorance (*L. argumentum ad ignorantiam*). Essentially, what this line of reasoning proposes is that if someone knows of no other explanation (or will not accept an alternative), then the one they reasoned to be true must be true. *That* approach is not science and must be rejected.

Thus, abiogenesis, the first of the three interlocking parts of evolution, *cannot* be *fact* based on evidence. It is instead nothing more than guesswork, speculation, and possibly even only wishful thinking about how life came to be. Without demonstrating abiogenesis, the entire Darwinian framework for the random, natural origin and diversity of life (evolution) becomes untenable—if life's beginning *cannot* be documented, then *no other part of the theory holds together* either according to Darwin's assumptions.

And as to whether abiogenesis could ever be demonstrated experimentally: Given the overwhelming complexity of the living cell, scientists will never create a fully functioning, irreducibly complex free-living cell through the random process of abiogenesis. Creation by God, rejected by science, is the *only* plausible explanation for the origin of life.

In the book of Nehemiah (Neh. 9:5–6), the Levite priests exhorted all Israel to praise the LORD for the wonder of Creation, saying (my emphasis),

> "Blessed be your glorious name, and may it be exalted above all blessing and praise. You alone are the LORD. You made the heavens, even the highest heavens, and all their starry host, the earth and all that is on it, the seas and all that is in

them. *You give life to everything,* and the multitudes of heaven worship you."

May we do the same.

## CHAPTER 4

# ADAPTATION (AKA DARWIN'S "NATURAL SELECTION")

Organisms are generally not limited to live in a highly specific set of conditions imposed on them by their environment. Typically, they can adapt to a variety of environments or growth conditions. Of course, some organisms are more limited to certain environments, whereas others are more widely adaptable depending on a variety of factors. *Adaptation* is the term properly used for the capacity of an organism to survive and thrive in several environments, and it depends entirely on the incredible amount of pre-existing information the DNA of organisms may contain, that is, their genomic potential.

However, you need to be aware that because it appears to provide evidence partially supporting Darwin's theory of Natural Selection, adaptation is often wrongly called evolution. This use of the word is misleading, because it muddies how evolution should properly be evaluated: the formation of new, entirely unique organisms, and especially groups of organisms, from those that already exist.

To get a good feel for the basics of adaptation, we need to know what DNA—what the genome—is potentially capable of doing. We do this first by briefly describing what we mean by DNA being *the* information molecule. Then we will use the awesome process of how it directs the formation of all the different kinds of cells (cell differentiation) to build the human body to show this ability. Third, we will explore the very large number of dog breeds as a clear example of the incredible amount of pre-existing information DNA might contain that would allow organisms to adapt. These parts form the biology foundation that allows adaptation to occur, and then with this information, we can understand and clearly distinguish it from evolution in the strict sense.

Finally, to see how adaptation works in the real world, we will look at a small insect, the soapberry bug. And, yes, the soapberry bug is really a bug, a "true bug" in terms of its biological classification. Why is it so special? Its importance lies in the fact that evolutionary biology showcases it as a clear, proven, unquestionable, and unambiguous example of rapid ("contemporary") evolution, evolution that has been observed both in nature and in the laboratory. The question we will be asking is this: Does the soapberry bug actually evolve in the strict sense, or should it more appropriately be said to simply adapt?

## DNA: THE INFORMATION MOLECULE

We have mentioned DNA a number of times up to this point. Now it's time to take a little closer look at one important aspect of it: the amount of information it contains. This amount of information—all of it already existing—is what allows an organism to adapt.

If you were to become involved with the in-depth study of the chemistry, biochemistry, structure, biological and physical interactions and functioning, all of which were integrated into the cell biology, molecular biology, and molecular genetics involved with DNA, you would be stepping into a huge and dynamic science field of biological research. Literally thousands of papers are published each month in multiple dozens of different science journals on this subject. These studies explore, analyze, dissect, and describe how DNA works at every level in virtually every known organism.

First off, I'm sure it would be no surprise if I told you that DNA is a very complex and not fully understood chemical molecule in terms of its functioning. But rather than describing and discussing its chemical structure, let's look at what it does, and we start that journey by again looking more closely at what a genome is. Recall that a genome is defined as (my emphasis) "an organism's complete set of DNA, including all of its genes, the functional units of heredity. Each genome contains *all of the information* needed to build and maintain that organism," and that genes are those parts of DNA that carry out its "instructions" to make proteins and other cell components. They do not operate independently apart from the information in DNA.

If we stop and consider that the genome made up of DNA has "all the information needed to build and maintain [an] organism," whether it is a bacterial cell, a dinosaur, or a human being, DNA becomes an absolutely amazing and critical molecule in its capacity to direct biological life. What this definition is saying is first that DNA directs *every* aspect of each individual cell's function. In addition, in organisms made up of more than one cell (such as us), DNA further functions by directing *all* the integrated interactions of each cell with every other cell, as well as directing how various cells respond to chemical signals from other cells (e.g., insulin regulation and release from the pancreas when it's needed). And, every aspect of DNA's role in building and maintaining life is purposeful—not random. *That* is indeed awesome!

The significance that every biochemical and physiological process is purposeful, integrated, and that none normally occurs independently from DNA's instructions is huge and fundamental. That biology—its homeostasis—constitutes the physiological foundation of any organism is a point that *cannot* be overemphasized.

The most important thing we need to consider about DNA is this: How much information might the DNA genome of an organism contain? If you look around you at the incredible diversity of the life you behold in nature, it can obviously be a lot. And, that is an understatement. The question becomes how best to present this concept to gain a true appreciation for the magnificence of the information capacity of this molecule. This is a case when referring to the numbers of various chemical components of DNA and their interactions—impressive as they might be (in the billions to tens of billions)—just doesn't do the job.

Rather, let's look at the two examples mentioned a few paragraphs ago of how DNA information can be *expressed* functionally. First, we'll see how the genome *builds* organisms from stem cells through the process called cell differentiation. Then, we'll use the astonishing variety of domestic dog breeds to give us an indication of the extent of pre-existing information that can be contained in DNA that might allow organisms to adapt to different environments and conditions without becoming new, unique animals. The principles we find in these examples directly apply to any plant or animal. Assuming that he was intellectually honest, Darwin would be hard pressed to claim he witnessed anything other than adaptation if he knew about DNA, the pre-existing information it contains, and the degree to which the genome maintains the stability of that information.

We talked briefly about genetic mistakes—mutations—earlier. Minor mutations in any organism, from simple viruses to bacteria to even more complex ones, could conceivably help the specific organism to adapt in some manner. They might conceivably even result in a new species coming into existence. More often, however, they tend to "degrade" the quality of that information and "disrupt function." They *cannot* begin to account for the entirely new genetic information needed to explain how the bewildering diversity of distinct organisms known today arose.

**The Genome Builds Organisms through Cell Differentiation.** Perhaps the best path to understanding how the genomic DNA information makes things happen is to look at the stem cell. Stem cells are currently a hot topic because they have so many potential uses in clinical medicine today. But what are they? Simply put, stem cells have two overriding characteristics: 1) They can and do divide into two cells ("daughter" cells), and 2) in that process of cell division, one of the daughter cells normally takes on new characteristics in size, shape, and function. This last process is known as "cell differentiation," and it is directly tied to the information in the genome's DNA being functionally "expressed" (i.e., producing a specific effect) through the cell's genes and their **alleles** (alternate forms of specific genes).

Typically when a human stem cell divides, one of two daughter cells remains a stem cell, of the same characteristics as the "parent" cell, to be able to divide again and maintain that particular cell line population. The other cell usually differentiates to some degree, and once it does, it cannot "de-differentiate" and return to its parental type under normal circumstances. Cancer cells are the exception. Because their genome's internal control mechanisms no longer fully govern cell division and differentiation according to signals received from the body, cancers operate independently to cause the chaos they do. However, under no conditions do they ever return to their parental stem cell type. Rather, they can de-differentiate further into more bizarre and aggressive types in some cancers.

However, for normal cells, the process of differentiation continues, producing stem cells that become ever more differentiated until arriving at the final cell type, which is known as "terminally differentiated." That final type makes up all the functioning tissues and organs you have.

For example, all of your blood cells—both red and white—are differentiated descendants of one particular stem cell type, a cell called a "hematoblast," through a process called **hematopoiesis**. Eventually, descendants of the hematoblast give rise to red cells, platelets, and all your different types of white blood cells. As is true in every other biological process, blood cell differentiation is directed by information contained in your genome's DNA, with various genes in the DNA being "turned on" or "turned off" from multiple protein and hormonal signals. These signals cause each of the hematoblast stem cells (and all other stem cells) involved to get the job done. Depending on the individual's needs, this process results in up to *one thousand billion* ($10^{11}$–$10^{12}$) new blood cells being produced daily. Like any other process designed to maintain your body's physiological stability, its homeostasis, you never have to think about whether hematopoiesis will work; it just does.

Continuing blood cell production is just one of the many jobs your body has carried out from the moment it became—your body.

In fact, homeostasis results in every cell type in your body having its own particular life span. Some cells are very long-lived (e.g., nerve, heart cells that live for years); others are relatively short-lived (e.g., the cells lining your small intestine, about 3 days). So, under normal conditions, all cells are fresh and ready to do the job they were designed to do. When their "time is up," they undergo the programmed physiological process of apoptosis in which they shut down, die, and are discarded or are reabsorbed. In this manner, every tissue and organ in your body is maintained.

And speaking of your body from the time it first started, perhaps the ultimate stem cell could be considered that which came to be at the moment your mother's ovum was fertilized. Recall again how a genome is defined:

> " . . . an organism's complete set of DNA, including all of its genes. Each genome contains all of the information needed to build and maintain that organism."

What does that definition imply for the fertilized ovum? Basically, it says that cell's DNA genome contained *every bit of information* to produce *every different type of cell, every different type of tissue* in your body as well as where they should go and how they should work. The list is extensive, but think for a moment of all the cells, tissues and functions of the brain, nerves, heart and circulatory system, lungs, muscles, tendons, bones, eyes, digestive tract, urinary and reproductive systems, among others. Every one in its place, doing the job it was designed to do at every moment of your life under normal conditions.

Your genome's DNA also determined what you would look like, how tall (or short) you would be, the color of your hair and eyes, and whether you would become a man or woman. And keep in mind that all of your biological self came to exist from genomic information passed on by your mother and father. When combined, that information produced you through the process of cell differentiation based on the DNA in the genome that was formed. It is beyond awe-inspiring that they all came from that one, first, fertilized cell and that information in DNA directed the whole process . . . no part of which is random.

Even more amazing, this process does not start from scratch. At fertilization, the ovum already contains all the necessary cellular machinery and chemical compounds for the DNA to do its job. Again, everything dealing with life is a continuing, purposeful, integrated whole, exactly the opposite of the conditions needed for evolution to occur.

And to think that God designed and created all of this process by His Word, then breathed *His* breath of life into us, giving us His life in our soul . . . (Gen. 2:7).

## GENOMIC POTENTIAL AND ADAPTATION

By now, you are aware that the potential amount of pre-existing genetic information DNA holds in the genome must be enormous. But, is this an actual biological fact, and does this biological fact—an organism's enormous genomic potential—have anything to do with its ability to adapt to its natural environment?

We will answer these questions by first looking at animal breeds in general, and then specifically, the domestic dog. Finally, we will discuss the soapberry bug, which you were introduced to earlier.

**Animal Breeds.** In considering animal breeds, we need to start with a brief, general background of what animal breeds are. Technically, a basic definition of a breed is "animals that, through selection and breeding, have come to resemble one another and pass those traits uniformly to their offspring." So, animals that exhibit some desirable trait are *purposefully* and *intentionally* bred with one another to continue and expand that trait.

How many animals might have breeds? The number is likely virtually unlimited. Breeds of fish, reptiles, birds (e.g., chickens, turkeys, geese) and many different mammals (e.g., cats, sheep, cows, goats) have all been reported. However, *never* forget that *any* type or breed of animal all belong to *one* specific genome, to *one* genetic pool of information, the DNA of the "parent" or "wild-type" animal.

Thinking about animal breeds can give us an even better feel for the potential of how much information DNA could contain. It almost seems that any animal purposefully bred to select certain characteristics by hobbyists or for domestic use can give rise to multiple different stable external characteristics. These include body types, body size, behavior, skin color patterns, and fur texture or length (in mammals) among many others. However, always keep in mind that what *cannot* change is anything that affects an organism's homeostasis—it must always maintain a stable physiological internal environment, regardless of what its external form is. Case in point—the domestic dog.

**Domestic Dog Breeds.** Dogs are not only companions but are also work animals, and some breeds can even be trained as service animals (e.g., to guide individuals with impaired sight). As is the case with *any* dog breed, however, "all dogs are of the *same* biological species," and therefore have the *same* genome. But, oh my—the information that that genome must contain!

To get a feel for this fact, let's begin with the known number of recognized dog breeds, comprehensively given as 231. Understand, however, that these are likely to represent only a *fraction* of the breeds known throughout the world when judged by the American Kennel Club (AKC) registry (over 150 breeds). Although other classifications are used, the AKC, consistent with most registries, divides breeds into seven groups. Each group has its own specific characteristics typical of all dogs within it in terms of behavior, herding and guarding ability, suitability as a pet, etc. Each breed, in turn, has its own particular characteristics. The AKC groups consist of:

- The Sporting Group (hunting and gun dogs)
- The Hound Group (scenthounds [e.g., the beagle]; sighthounds [e.g., the greyhound])
- The Working Group (guarding, sledding, rescue, protection)

- The Terrier Group (breeds originally developed to kill ground vermin)
- The Toy Group (miniaturized versions of dogs from other groups)
- The Non-Sporting Group (also, the companion group)
- The Herding Group (dogs that instinctively control movements of animals)

In weight, dogs range from the tiny Chihuahua (required to be not bigger than 6 lbs) to the very large Mastiff (175–190 lbs). In heat/cold tolerance, dogs range from the ancient Pharaoh Hound of the Mideast (short coat; tolerates heat but not cold) to the Alaskan Malamute (long, full coat; tolerates cold but not heat). And as to size, we go back to the Chihuahua (6" to 9" paw to shoulder) compared to the Great Dane (up to 30" paw to shoulder). What enormous differences we see, not only in the weights, heat/cold tolerance, and sizes of these dogs, but in the characteristics, behaviors, and uses of individual breeds as well as breed groups.

Now, here's the important point: Always keep in mind that *all* the genetic information responsible for the purposeful development of this incredible variety of dog breeds (as well as breeds of other animals) *pre-exists* in the DNA of the "dog" genome . . . all of it, and that the remarkable differences between breeds result from recombinations of chromosomes causing various genes and their different forms (their alleles) to be expressed (or not)! At the same time, I have not found recorded anywhere that a *new*, dog-like animal ever developed (evolved) from such breeding, despite the likely extensive environmental stresses involved in it. As for any other genome, core information in the genome of the dog remains stable and produces a dog regardless, as is the case with any other organism.

This principle of genomic stability stands in stark contrast to the mountain of new information needed from purposeless, random genetic events to produce the awe-inspiring variety of plants and animals we have on planet Earth. And, one last point: The number and variety of animal breeds that have been developed shows that in the wild, organisms clearly have the ability to *adapt* to their environment (consistent with Darwin's theory of Natural Selection) without the need to *evolve*.

The bottom line is that any organism's genome—any organism—contains an extravagant amount of genetic information to help it cope with and adapt to its environment. Adaptation is a real biological phenomenon.

**The Soapberry Bug: A Case Study Demonstrating Contemporary "Evolution"?** If you were to go online and combine the search terms *soapberry bug* with *evolution*, you would find literally hundreds of references to this fascinating little insect. It is used by evolutionary biology as a prime and uncontested example to demonstrate with "direct evidence" not only that evolution has taken place but that it takes place today. Because of this position, evolution can claim that the soapberry bug documents and helps validate the theory of evolution.

General references to the soapberry bug (e.g., Soapberry Bugs of the World) characterize it as "rapidly evolving," "adaptively evolving," and as demonstrating "contemporary evolution," or "adaptive evolution." It is also featured in evolutionary biology textbooks, such as *Evolution*. Because of its importance to evolution proponents, we need to spend a little time with it.

In terms of its biology, it is actually classified as—a bug. In fact, it is included in a group of insects known as the "true bugs" (taxonomic Order Hemiptera). It is quite small. Various species range anywhere from a just over a quarter inch (~7 mm) to a little over one-half inch (~15 mm) long. It gets its name because it feeds on the fruit of certain members of the family of the soapberry plants. It does so by penetrating the fleshy outer covering of the soapberry fruit with its mouthparts (its beak) to feed on the seeds inside.

What exactly interests evolutionary biologists about the soapberry bug? Field observations have documented that the length of the soapberry bug's beak matches the depth of soapberry fruit flesh it has to penetrate to get to the seeds. Specifically, beak length varies over generations according to the soapberry fruit available. In other words, thin-fleshed soapberry fruits result in populations of soapberry bugs with short beaks; thick-fleshed fruits give rise to populations of bugs with longer beaks. Such evidence is presented as being right in line with and supporting Darwin's theory of Natural Selection and especially evolution. Pretty neat, right?

But, there's more. Sophisticated, very carefully designed, and well performed laboratory studies, *fully consistent with how science is done*, have shown that when colonies of bugs with short beaks are moved to fruit with thick flesh, their beaks get longer over succeeding generations. Beaks of separately maintained parental colonies and fed on the original thinner-fleshed soapberry fruit do not change. And, when colonies with "evolved" longer beaks are moved back to thin-fleshed fruits, their beaks get shorter again in succeeding generations, confirming field studies. And all of these changes are believed to *not* be due to mutations, but to characteristics that pre-exist in their genetic makeup. So, the soapberry bug clearly demonstrates evolution by evolution's standards, agreed? And because of such studies, evolution can not only be considered a fact, but a very much alive, active scientific field, right?

Not necessarily.

The soapberry bug is an instance where comparing the evidence with evolution's standards for evolution becomes vague, fuzzy, and shapeless. Recall the very broad, all-encompassing definition of evolution given by evolutionary biology we talked about earlier, that if there's *any* genetic component involved (even due to a shift in shape of certain genes [ie., alleles] in a cell), then what happens can be called evolution? Accordingly, if the soapberry bug actually demonstrated evolution according to that definition, then science standards require that changes in the soapberry bug's genetic components *be documented* at the same time as they are occurring. These changes would have to correlate with changes in its beak length and be reproduced experimentally. However, *no such changes were actually demonstrated in those studies, only inferred* from the changes in its beak length based on previous studies.

Far more importantly, however, *no new, unique, soapberry bug-like organisms have ever "evolved" from the soapberry bug's feeding habits in the laboratory or in nature.* The soapberry bug has always remained . . . the soapberry bug. Therefore, no evolution.

A more reasonable and defensible explanation is that, given the potentially huge amount of pre-existing genetic information an organism has (i.e., its genomic potential as demonstrated by the astonishing variety of dog and other animal breeds), the soapberry bug's beak length changes should be more appropriately inferred to be adaptation.

## ADAPTATION—THE BOTTOM LINE

Where does all this biology lead us? To validating Charles Darwin's theory of Natural Selection, but only within *very restricted limits.* Darwin's *documented* observations, *not* any theories coming from them, are *completely consistent* with organisms *adapting* to their surroundings due to their pre-existing genetic information. Further, because of that pre-existing genetic information, adaptation can and should be considered a fact, a real biologic phenomenon.

However, keep clearly in mind that the phenomenon of adaptation does *not* demonstrate evolution as this term should be strictly be defined: no new organisms have ever been demonstrated to result from such studies.

In terms of science, simply saying the soapberry bug or any other organism evolved without such specific evidence to support that claim does not make it so.

In the next four chapters, we now turn our attention to evolution in its most strict sense—how new animals are presumed to arise from existing ones.

## CHAPTER 5

# EVOLUTION'S ACHILLES' HEEL: HOMEOSTASIS

*"What I cannot create, I do not understand."*

Nobel-prize-winning physicist Dr. Richard Feynman

I never cease to be amazed at how life's processes are so complex, interactive, intricate, dynamic, and vital beyond understanding. I also stand in awe at how purposeful, self-regulating, and interconnected all life processes are; not one occurs in isolation from any other, and every one affects every other in every organism and from organism to organism. Although biologists routinely study even the smallest life process isolated from others to accurately characterize it, they must *always* take account of *"how"* the process is integrated into every other life process of an organism. This integration can only be accomplished through the holistic principle of **homeostasis** in terms of the organism's physiology.

Applying the principle of homeostasis to evolution results in a near death sentence to the theory that new organisms can and do arise (evolve) from existing ones. Curiously, evolution theory does not address, explain, or take into account either homeostasis or an organism's physiology in asserting the certainty that new organisms can and do arise from existing ones. And yet, these two biologic principles form the foundation of every life process in every organism known.

The critical point of knowing about homeostasis is that no organism that has ever existed, presently exists, or ever will exist is exempt from the absolute need for internal, integrated control of all its life processes. So, no plant, no bacterial type, no protozoan, no sponge, no jellyfish, no mosquito or crab, not the largest or smallest dinosaur, nor any mammal (including us) can live without its internal environment being tightly controlled within certain limits. And how big were the largest and smallest dinosaurs? The largest complete dinosaur fossil belongs to the enormous *Brachiosaurus*, an animal about four stories high and the length of two large school busses. The smallest belongs to *Compsognathus*, slightly larger than a chicken. No matter—their homeostasis would have to have been maintained during their evolution.

Maintaining homeostasis is the absolute foundation for biological life.

And the principle of homeostasis began with the nineteenth century French physiologist Claude Bernard.

## HOMEOSTASIS: THE *"MILIEU INTÉRIEUR"*

At the time I was working on my PhD in Zoology, all doctoral candidates had to pass a set of seven "preliminary exams" (or simply prelims) to qualify for formally entering the doctoral program. The prelims were divided into four major exams of three hours each and three minor exams of two hours each, all given in a two-week period. Each exam covered one of your core biological study areas in as much detail as the professor cared to explore. There were no holds barred as to what was asked, and you either passed the exam or had to retake it. One such major area for me was mammalian physiology—and that exam covered anything we had learned in the year-long course, as well as in the massive textbooks we used.

I was used to taking exams with specific essay questions, which addressed several important areas that we had studied. That was not to be the case with mammalian physiology.

I walked into the classroom where the exam was given, the professor greeted me by asking if I was ready, and after I said yes, he handed me my three exam booklets and placed a single sheet of paper upside down on the table in front of me. When I turned it over, I saw but one question: "Discuss Claude Bernard's *milieu intérieur* with respect to mammalian physiology."

That was it. I had never come across the phrase *milieu intérieur* before, nor had we discussed it or Claude Bernard in class. After panicking for a moment, I guessed at a rough translation as possibly being "interior environment." Then, based on what we had studied, I further guessed that what I was being asked was to show how physiology worked to keep the whole of an organism's functions in balance; that is, discuss homeostasis. Fortunately, I was right. I wrote steadily for the entire three hours and did pass the exam.

As a result, I gained an enormous respect for the physiologic principle of homeostasis that has remained with me from that time on.

**Claude Bernard.** Claude Bernard was the first biologist who appreciated the holistic nature of life. In that regard, he is credited as being the first "systems biologist," someone who studied life's processes not in isolation from one another but as an integrated whole, where every one would affect every other. In the mid- to late 1800s, he proposed and demonstrated that an organism's ability to live and function required an internal environment that remained constant, stable, and within set limits. Today this principle of the stability of life is known as homeostasis, which roughly translated means a state of steady (-stasis) equilibrium (homeo-).

Although Bernard originally applied the principle of homeostasis to certain organ systems of the whole animal (pancreas and liver function), today it is absolutely clear that it is the underlying principle for any life that exists to thrive. It applies equally to *any* multi-celled organism or *any* individual free-living cell, whether it is a bacterial cell or a single-celled animal (i.e., a protozoan, like an amoeba).

Evolution points to parasitic organisms such as viruses because they do not maintain their own environment; thus, evolution proponents would argue that homeostasis is not a universal principle. However, such organisms either completely or partially *depend on their host* to provide the specific, stable environment as well as all the biochemical machinery they need in order to survive and reproduce.

**How Homeostasis Works.** Bernard's concept of homeostasis was revolutionary to the manner in which biological function was viewed at the time. Never before had it been proposed that the internal stability of an organism could *only* be maintained through some sort of purposeful feedback, feedback both from the external environment in which an organism lived as well as within its internal environment.

It further implied that this feedback could only work by simultaneously affecting multiple, interacting, fully integrated control mechanisms to keep the internal environment stable and in balance. No process could operate independently from any other. When one became active and increased (or decreased) its activity, others that were affected would respond accordingly.

All this really exquisite, purposeful feedback on an organism's functioning would take place continually, regardless of the physiological systems involved. None of it is in any way random. None of it.

This brief description incorporates the whole of homeostasis. Now we will turn to actual biology to make this principle real and show that, in sharp contrast to evolution, it is solid science. Although we will use just a few examples, homeostasis has been found and demonstrated in every form of life studied.

**Brief Examples from the Whole Organism.** To gain some understanding of this principle as it actually works, let's look at two examples from ourselves (the human body) at a top level to begin to get a glimpse of the delicate workings of homeostasis within our own normal physiological systems. They will be described only sufficiently to make the point needed of its interactive complexity. These examples are:

- water balance
- core body temperature

How many human systems are affected by homeostasis? The answer is: all of them. So, the number is enormous, but quickly looking at certain various lab values in the blood work obtained as part of a routine physical exam can give you some idea of their extent. These data would include red and white blood cell numbers (WBCs in their various types), blood cell sizes, red cell hemoglobin levels; kidney function information, and blood electrolytes (e.g., sodium, potassium). Other tests could be done to evaluate how much oxygen and carbon dioxide ($O_2$, $CO_2$) your blood contained, etc. Under normal conditions each and every one of these systems and every other is maintained in specific limits by homeostatic mechanisms in your body.

**1. Water Balance:** If you drink too much water, your kidneys get rid of the excess; if you drink too little or lose water (e.g., while sweating), your body secretes a factor to make them retain water from being eliminated. The kidneys do this to keep, as far as possible, the hydration, salt, and mineral levels of your tissues (not to mention the fluidity of your blood) constant and within normal limits.

This action centers on the multiple effects of a hormone (vasopressin; antidiuretic hormone, "ADH") within the kidney. The normal mammalian body "knows," by various, multiple feedback mechanisms, what its proper fluid balance must be and responds accordingly under all circumstances to keep it that way. It does so first by activating or shutting down appropriate control mechanisms that lead to increased or decreased ADH production, which results in increased/decreased urine elimination. This process is homeostasis in action.

**2. Core Body Temperature:** What about your normal (core) body temperature of 98.6°F (37°C)? You know if you were to exercise strenuously or remained out in the sunshine on a hot summer's day, you build up heat. One of the ways your body responds to becoming too warm is by sweating; the sweat evaporates and cools you. But, as you would expect from the first example, your kidneys will likely retain more water to compensate for that lost in sweating.

But that's not all. To further help get rid of the extra heat at the same time as you increase sweating, more capillaries in your skin open so more blood will circulate in them to radiate excess heat away, and you might look "flushed" as a result. The increased surface area also helps cool you with sweating, and both mechanisms work together to maintain your core body temperature.

Again, your body knows when it might be too warm or cool through multiple feedback mechanisms and responds accordingly. However, if you were outside on a cold day and your body were to start getting too cool, the opposite happens: you might sweat only minimally (if at all!) and the capillaries in your skin would start closing to keep your blood in your core to maintain core temperature.

Only birds and mammals have the physiological ability to internally regulate their core body temperature within tight limits through their metabolic processes. Technically, this capacity is known as homeothermia, and animals having this capacity are commonly thought of as *warm-blooded*. In contrast, animals that can *not* internally regulate their core body temperatures (such as reptiles) have variable and wide-ranging body temperatures that depend on those of their environment and the amount of their muscle mass. These animals are known as poikilotherms (Gk. *poikilo-*, "variable"). Interestingly, although reptiles are commonly thought of as cold-blooded, some (such as the 2,000 lb. leatherback sea turtle) can generate heat from their very large muscle mass when they use it, a warm-blooded characteristic, but even so, they cannot *regulate* their body temperatures. The exact same principle would directly apply to large dinosaurs that have been called warm-blooded. None could internally control their body temperature.

So, now you have an idea of how homeostasis works in the whole organism. But, what about individual cells?

**3. Example from the Cell**. As does the whole organism, so does the individual cell (either free-living or one of a multi-celled organism) rigorously maintain its own internal environment. Perhaps the best way to illustrate this point is by noting how tightly protein production is regulated within a cell for its own use or to export it. The number of proteins produced by any cell type is incredibly varied and enormous—but for any *single* protein, that protein is produced only *when* it is needed, in the *amount* it is needed, and for the *duration* of time it is needed, whether it is used within the cell or exported. If it remains in the cell, the cell machinery then degrades it and gets rid of the waste products at the proper time, according to the instructions it receives from its regulatory mechanisms, especially the information in DNA.

Pretty neat? I think so! But, always keep in mind that evolution says that these intricate, interlinked processes are all the result of *random* events setting them up in the first place . . .

## HOMEOSTASIS: THE BOTTOM LINE

Homeostasis—an internal physiological environment that stays stable with all processes in equilibrium—is needed in the most utter and absolute sense for any life to maintain itself and thrive. Because *all* physiological systems are interdependent, if just *one* physiologic system is permanently altered to the smallest degree (e.g., by a "positive" mutation that might lead to evolution), then all other systems would at least have to be immediately capable of compensating for that change. If the change that occurred were significant . . . all other systems would *have to change simultaneously* in a *non-random, integrated manner* to accommodate it.

Thus, homeostasis becomes *the* far-reaching core physiological principle that is *the* essential foundation to the survival and thriving of any plant, bacterial, or animal life form. It is the biological equivalent of a philosophical "first principle," something that is self-evident and does not require reasoning to establish it, something that is physically an absolute foundation—in this case for life itself.

How does this physiological principle apply to evolution?

In the case of both a positive, *minor* random mutation as well as a *major* one (or set of ones), the animal in which these occurred could not wait for the necessary other random mutations to happen to bring all of its affected physiologic systems up to speed, to synchronize them with the initial change. All changes would have to occur virtually immediately and simultaneously. Otherwise, the animal's internal physiological environment would become unstable and would no longer be in equilibrium. And if that outcome should happen? Not only would the animal not thrive, but its vitality would be degraded at the least; more likely, it would die.

The problem: Could all affected physiologic systems change simultaneously as required? The answer is: No. That such integrated changes could *ever* take place simultaneously is literally impossible, because evolution mandates that all such changes must occur—*randomly*. Recall what random implies for evolution, "that its process must be considered, in the most complete and *absolute* sense, to be *utterly* without any:

- purpose, direction, or pattern
- predictable order (i.e., it is disorderly)
- plan, outcome, or objective
- conscious input or influence"

Homeostasis is the biological requirement that locks any animal's descendants into being the same essential animal as was their ancestor, just as we found with the soapberry bug.

So, where does homeostasis leave evolution as science and fact? As far as science is concerned, evolution would have to demonstrate with definitive, direct evidence 1) that one animal could actually evolve to an entirely different animal and 2) specifically show how, on the basis of random mutations, homeostasis was preserved. Until that happens, the theory of evolution cannot be considered fact. In fact . . .

The biological first principle of homeostasis is the Achilles' heel of evolution.

# CHAPTER 6

# EVOLUTION'S BIOLOGICAL CHALLENGE

Evolution claims that it has been tested according to the scientific method and that such testing has shown this theory to be a valid explanation for how all life came to be that has ever existed. Thus, it is claimed to have met *philosophical* (not applied) science standards and more especially, that fossils, DNA similarities, and other circumstantial evidence confirm it as "fact." Such standards appear to be based on a philosophical discipline known as "philosophical naturalism," which teaches that the natural world is all that there is. This position has nothing to do with any science that evolution could claim.

However, if evolution in fact were to have met the criteria of the scientific method as it asserts, what's the problem? That is, why shouldn't Creation just fold up its tent and go home?

The answer? It hasn't. *None* of the testing evolution claims as validating it addresses the *core* biologic issue: the biological *process* of how one animal evolves to another in light of the absolute need to maintain homeostasis. Evolution offers not one bit of direct evidence gained by experiment to support its assertion that one existing animal can ever, in fact, randomly evolve to a new, unique one that has never been seen before. Not one bit. And in doing that, it effectively exempts itself from the rigors of the scientific method that requires direct evidence.

Thus, the critical challenge to evolutionary biology is that it must *demonstrate* the *process* of evolution with direct evidence to meet science standards in the same manner as abiogenesis would have to do.

And what is the direct evidence needed in this particular case? Namely, purposefully evolving one *living* organism into another unlike the first through experimental manipulation of DNA at a minimum. The evolved animal would have to be sufficiently different in terms of its internal and external anatomy and physiology to make it unique, and it would have to be demonstrated to be as such. Simply asserting that the philosophical tests used to validate the theory of evolution "need not involve laboratory experiments" is not sufficient. Results from that experimental demonstration would have to meet at least three absolute criteria to be considered potentially applicable:

1.  The new organism would have to have been postulated to be a direct descendant of an existing one if two living organisms were used for the test. A more definitive test would have to yield a new, never before described species, the lowest rank of biological classification.

2.  In either case, the new organism would not crossbreed or hybridize with the existing one or any other species to produce offspring that would then be able to reproduce additional progeny.

3.  Finally, the confirming test would subject the two species to the procedure of interspecies cloning, where the DNA of one species is inserted into the egg of another, and no viable organisms would result.

Be aware that even if this approach were successful, it would only be the *beginning* of gaining evidence supporting the biology of evolution. Given that evolution's foundation is the *random* mutation being selected by Natural Selection, the entire set of studies would have to be redone incorporating randomness into the experimental design to gain the new genetic information required for a new organism.

## EVOLUTION REQUIRES NEW GENETIC INFORMATION

At this point, it certainly seems obvious that evolution of any new animal would require new genomic information as Dr. Meyer has so well stated, otherwise you would simply wind up with a variation of an existing one. However, were you to consult an evolution text or reference book on this point, the first issue you would find to deal with is, in fact, "What does evolution biology mean by *new information?*"

Good question. Evolution cites changing color patterns of various animals or the length of dorsal spines on certain stickleback fish as demonstrating new genetic information. And let's not forget about the soapberry bug that is said to evolve because its beak length changes in response to its food source. However, without direct evidence of unique, random genetic changes *that are specifically predicted by sequence and type* in any experimental design to test it, these examples sound rather like simple adaptive responses based on mix-and-match combinations of pre-existing genetic information at fertilization that select for the trait needed.

Sound familiar? Think back to dog breeds for a moment. Recall that all dog breeds are of the same biologic genus and species (*Canis familiaris*). The over 231 known breeds all result from mix-and-match interactions of pre-existing information in the dog genome. Just as no new dog breed results from any "new" information this process produces, the different color patterns in moths (and other examples) would certainly be consistent with pre-existing genetic information allowing adaptation of these animals to their surroundings.

But what did Dr. Meyer specifically ask that was so direct and revolutionary, and how did its emphasis differ from evolution's examples you just read? Note carefully again his question when he was interviewed by author Lee Strobel: "Where did the information come from to build all these *new* [unique] *proteins, cells,* and *body plans?*" Recall that he was referring to the *new* genetic information that would be required to produce *new* proteins, *new* cells, *new* body plans . . . without that information, unique, never–seen-before organisms evolving from existing ones could never occur. And, all these changes would have had to take place through independent random events.

So, just how does evolution explain the process through which new organisms come to be? All evolution is proposed to be driven by 1) natural selection that "alone *creates* complex . . . organisms," and 2) mutations, without which "there would be no evolution." Other genetic events (e.g., rearrangements of genes or alleles, recombination during fertilization, etc.) are also considered necessary to achieve the variation needed for natural selection.

*But* at the same time, processes other than natural selection "tend to degrade the fitness of the organism," and mutations in particular "tend to disrupt function" (as would be expected because they impact homeostasis) "if they have any effect at all." So, mutations are really a "good news, bad news" foundation for evolution, even if it ignores the roadblock of homeostasis.

## HOMEOSTASIS' CHALLENGE TO EVOLUTION

It is clear that evolution 1) has *no* explanation 2) documented with definitive direct evidence 3) that supports *any* process showing how a new animal arises from an existing one. According to evolution, new information can only come from mutations. But in evolutionary theory (based on natural events that occur entirely apart from God's purposefulness), all mutations must be random. Is there a problem here? Absolutely.

What random implies for evolution is that all "positive" mutations, rare as they might be, will produce changes *independently* of any other mutation. There can be no integration or linking, because they are random. In terms of biology, preserving homeostasis and the negative fallout from any random mutations are mutually exclusive. If a mutation should occur that produced a change in a physiologic system, other systems would likely not accommodate that change. Not only would the organism no longer thrive, it would most likely die.

How would evolution have to work in the real world? We talked about the need for genetic changes causing evolution to never disturb homeostasis in the process, to never upset the functioning of any organ system from changes in another. Yet any changes to an animal causing it to evolve to a new animal would have to be random. Does this hurdle seem like an impossible task?

The answer: It is, and the giraffe is a perfect example of it, which we will discuss next.

## CHAPTER 7

# THE GIRAFFE: *THE* PROTOTYPE EXAMPLE FOR REJECTING EVOLUTION

The speculated evolution of the giraffe is a clear, clean prototype example in a living animal of the biological problems inherent in evolution. No distinct, unique animal on the face of the earth (past or present) could ever have avoided some of the same kinds of issues the giraffe would have had to go through to evolve as it did. Additionally, the giraffe's evolution highlights the hard limitations of *inferring* evolution from indirect evidence, especially the claimed increasingly complex fossils appearing over time.

The interpretation of fossil evidence involved in the giraffe's evolution is highly controversial in terms of giraffe's genealogy, because any investigator who studies it finds many gaps and the equivalent of "missing links." That said, *no* ancestral path for the giraffe's evolution has been identified with certainty, despite claims to the contrary. The only point most evolution investigators seem to agree on is that the giraffe evolved from a deer-sized, short-necked ancestor to the tall, stocky animal it is today. On the surface, this explanation sounds plausible and is certainly in line with the teachings of Darwinian evolution.

Biologically, however, the convoluted and related steps the giraffe would have had to go through to evolve in that manner reminds me of the classic nursery rhyme about "The House That Jack Built." As you read about the giraffe, consider how this rhyme could reflect that process as it builds one stanza on another (I've included only five of the eleven stanzas to illustrate the point).

## THIS IS THE HOUSE THAT JACK BUILT

*This is the house that Jack built*

*This is the malt*
*That lay in the house that Jack built.*

*This is the rat*
*That ate the malt*
*That lay in the house that Jack built.*

*This is the cat*
*That killed the rat*
*That ate the malt*
*That lay in the house that Jack built.*

*This is the dog*
*That worried the cat*
*That killed the rat*
*That ate the malt*
*That lay in the house that Jack built.*

I'm sure you get the idea of how one thing builds on and impacts something else in this nursery rhyme. So, now for a preview of what applying that process to the giraffe's evolution might mean: Step-wise evolution of a long neck from a short-necked, deer-sized ancestor would require a higher **blood pressure** each time the neck lengthened to push the blood up the longer neck into the brain. Each step's increase in blood pressure would, in turn, require modifications to the whole cardiovascular system (heart and blood vessels), so nothing would be damaged by the increasing blood pressures. Those changes, in turn, would require changes in the tissues of every organ and other tissues in the body to accommodate the increased blood pressure.

Evolutionary theory asserts that mutations are the only way new genetic information can enter the genome and produce evolution of new animals, the survival of which would be decided by Darwin's "Natural Selection." Because changes to so many organs would be involved in the case of the giraffe's lengthening neck, mutations would have to happen *in sets*, and the sets would have to evolve virtually simultaneously so that the giraffe's homeostasis would not be disturbed—no exceptions. If any one change took place out of sequence or ahead of another, homeostasis would be violated and that ancestral giraffe line would never survive. That's biology. It's ironic that that survival/non-survival situation is also the foundational requirement mandated by Darwin's "Natural Selection."

Also, keep in mind during this discussion that although mutations are the only way to produce new genetic information leading to evolution, they "tend to disrupt function" " . . . if they have any effect at all." And worse (for evolution), each positive mutation in a set required for lengthening the giraffe's neck, blood pressure, and associated changes would have to come about . . . *randomly.* No time factor could be involved, nor could one mutation be linked to or influenced by another.

Evolution proclaims that all life originated from and can be explained by random events producing new animals. The impossibility of the giraffe's evolution will show what happens when you not only apply science properly, but take evolution at its word that random mutations power the entire process: It doesn't work.

Now, a few points of specific information about the giraffe's biology to illustrate and emphasize the problems its "House That Jack Built" evolution would have had to overcome.

## GIRAFFE OVERVIEW

The giraffe is an amazing animal, not only in terms of how it looks, but especially in terms of its biology. For our purposes, its most striking external feature is its long neck, which can range anywhere from 6.5 to nearly 8 feet above its body. When its body is factored in, the giraffe stands 14-19 feet tall, with females not being quite as tall as males. Its remarkable height allows it to feed on leaves of branches fairly high off the ground. In that manner, the giraffe is said to have a distinct Darwinian "competitive advantage" over other plant-eating animals in its local, dry environment (presumably having evolved this way according to the tenets of "Natural Selection"). Giraffes live 15-25 years in the wild, but can live up to 32-40 years in captivity.

The adult giraffe's long neck is not due to it having more neck (cervical) vertebrae; it has seven, the same number as other mammals. Rather, its neck is long because the adult giraffe's cervical vertebrae grow to be strikingly longer than those of other mammals from the time it is born. The giraffe is proposed to have evolved as it has because its ancestor's diet *may* have contained "toxins that caused higher mutation rates and [therefore] a higher rate of evolution."

As interesting and important as its long neck is by itself in the giraffe's evolution, the feature we're going to look at most closely is the one said to have **coevolved** along with its neck: the highest blood pressure of any animal known.

From an evolutionary standpoint—why would the giraffe need high blood pressure? Because of its long neck and to overcome the effects of gravity, the giraffe's heart would have to have evolved to push blood up about six feet to the brain under high enough pressure to reach and nourish it. Despite assertions to the contrary, it is just this aspect of the giraffe that evolution has no adequate explanation for. In fact, the giraffe's blood pressure is just the tip of the iceberg of adjustments in its anatomy and physiology needed to accommodate its high blood pressure.

This section will call out some major issues involved in the giraffe's blood pressure point-by-point, so you can understand more clearly the enormity of the challenge to evolution this animal poses. Beyond that, you will be ready to see how the challenges evolution faces here are almost trivial compared with those needed for the evolution of reptiles to mammals.

Before beginning this section, please read the disclaimer immediately following.

**Disclaimer:** Human blood pressure information in this section was obtained online from the American Heart

Association, the Mayo Clinic, The Centers for Disease Control (CDC), and other sources. This section was designed to provide basic information that *specifically* applies to evolution's problems in the giraffe. Hypertension in humans is a complex medical issue, and you are encouraged to talk to your medical professional about any questions or concerns the information in this section might raise.

## BLOOD PRESSURE OVERVIEW

We begin here with definitions so that all terms can be used correctly and in context.

**Blood Pressure Terms.** What, exactly, do we mean by "normal"? You might think that there would be a specific, clear, precise definition, but there is not, not in biology. Rather, "normal" refers to a middle value between upper and lower limits, for example, an animal's blood pressure, for those that have a blood pressure. So, technically, a human or any animal that has blood pressure measurements *within accepted limits* for that particular species is said to be *normotensive*, that is, it has a *normal* blood pressure. On the other hand, if blood pressure measurements are consistently *above* normal limits, that condition is termed *hypertensive*, the prefix "hyper-" meaning "above" or "excessive." What if blood pressure measurements are consistently *below* normal limits? If that occurs, this state is known as *hypotensive*, the prefix "hypo-" meaning "below" or "beneath."

In more general usage, the point to keep clearly in mind as we talk about the giraffe is that either "hyper-" or "hypo-" applied to *any* condition in biology or medicine indicates a condition that lies outside of an *established normal standard* based on established limits for that condition, and therefore indicates an abnormal, possibly diseased state.

Two values are used to report blood pressure in mammals: the systolic, reported first, is the higher of the two and reflects the pressure in the arteries at the level of the heart when it beats (contracts). The lower of the two is the diastolic and reflects arterial pressure between beats when the heart relaxes and refills with blood. Either refers to the pressure it takes to push a column of mercury (Hg) upwards a certain distance, measured in millimeters (mm).

**Examples of Normal Blood Pressures.** Although normal mammalian blood pressure values are specific to each animal as you might expect, curiously they are reported to not vary widely, whether we are talking about mice, rats, horses, or humans. For example, human blood pressures of 120/80 mm Hg or less are considered normal. Those of a resting normal blood pressures of a horse range from 110–120/70 mm Hg, not terribly different, whereas dogs have somewhat higher normal blood pressures of 140/75 mm Hg.

Now, what about the giraffe?

## THE GIRAFFE'S CARDIOVASCULAR SYSTEM AND EVOLUTION

To understand the giraffe better, we need to look at certain specialized functions and features of the giraffe's cardiovascular system, and what these imply to its speculated evolution. We will do so in three parts:

- First, its high but normal blood pressure and whether the giraffe's organs show signs of hypertension (technically: hypertension **sequelae**) as would be found in humans
- Second, features of its neck that allow it to lower its head and drink, then raise it without becoming faint from blood rushing down its neck into its body
- Third, what these two characteristics imply to homeostasis requirements for the giraffe's evolution

**The Giraffe's Blood Pressure**. In striking contrast to humans and other animals, the adult giraffe's *normal* blood pressure is 210-325/180 mm Hg, a level needed to push the blood up from the heart the 6 feet or so to the brain. The giraffe is not born with a long neck and high blood pressure. Rather the giraffe's blood pressure increases as its neck becomes longer while it grows to adulthood. Interestingly, the giraffe's heart is reported to be no larger than would be expected for its body size, but produces the high blood pressure needed because of a very high heart rate (about 170 beats/minute; human normal is 60–100) and stronger left heart wall.

How high is the giraffe's blood pressure compared to that of a human? Consider the possible consequences if a human were to have the giraffe's blood pressure. In a human, two closely taken consecutive blood pressure readings of 180/120 mm Hg or greater could constitute a hypertensive *emergency* (hypertensive crisis) requiring *immediate* medical attention; at the least, stroke and organ damage to the heart, eyes, and kidneys all could result very quickly. Further, consistent human blood pressure readings of 140–160/90–100 mm Hg usually indicate some level of hypertension, which, in an untreated patient over time, could lead to heart enlargement and failure, kidney failure, failure of the aorta (the major artery leading from the heart to the rest of the body), stroke, and arteriosclerosis, among other disease issues. We will particularly look at kidney failure shortly.

As for the giraffe? The giraffe is not bothered by its high blood pressure but *requires* it for its blood to reach its brain when it is standing upright. Biologically, what this fact implies is that the *whole* cardiovascular system and *every* organ it distributes blood to not only fully accommodates that blood pressure but is not damaged by it. And, keep in mind that this is the *normal* situation.

What does this biology imply? Evolution theory would require that the giraffe's genome would have to have randomly evolved simultaneously in at least *five* ways. First, the anatomic information to direct growth of its long neck from its speculated short-necked ancestor would have to have evolved. Second, genomic information would also have to have simultaneously coevolved increased blood pressure each time the giraffe's ancestor's neck grew longer to ensure blood reaching the brain. Third, in response to the increased blood pressure, the entire cardiovascular system would then have to have simultaneously coevolved to accommodate it without damage. Fourth, every organ would have to have coevolved to not be damaged by the high blood pressure.

The last two requirements are absolutely critical, because the increasing blood pressure would affect every artery and vein, heart function, kidneys, the giraffe's brain as well as all associated blood vessels. Why the brain? The giraffe's brain blood pressure (normally around 100 mm Hg) *doubles* when it bends down to drink. And fifth and last, the tight, non-elastic skin of its six-foot legs would also have had to coevolve to help move blood back up to its heart from its feet so tissue fluid (edema) would not build up there.

For organ function in the giraffe, let's focus on one particular example of many: the required coevolution of its kidneys to handle its high blood pressure. To help understand the giraffe's situation, we will again start with what can happen to the kidneys in human hypertension.

Kidneys require high volumes of blood to flow through them to nourish and enable them to filter out body wastes from the blood. Untreated chronic hypertension in humans can cause the arteries feeding the kidneys to weaken, narrow, or harden, reducing that blood flow. Reduced blood flow damages the kidney's filtering units (the glomeruli), which in turn reduces their ability not only to filter wastes but also to regulate the body's fluid, acid, and salt levels along with other essential kidney functions (such as helping regulate blood pressure). As you can probably guess, the list you just read describes only a few changes at a top level; the detail involved is far more intricate and complex.

Now, what about the giraffe's kidneys? Do they shows signs of hypertension-related kidney damage as would be found in humans? The short answer is no, but they should.

Because they are at the same level in its body as the heart, the giraffe's kidneys would bear the full brunt of its 210–325/180 mm Hg blood pressure, yet they show no signs of hypertension as are found in the human. Rather, they are considered to have "a *species-specific* evolutionary adaptation" (another required coevolution event) that would allow them to function properly. This "adaptation" turns out to be an extraordinarily tough renal capsule (the membrane covering of the kidney) that is greater than *10-fold stronger* than those of other mammals, which is said to allow the kidney to function normally. Whether this is the definitive answer for their ability to withstand the giraffe's high blood pressure is not clear. What is clear is that the kidney's filtering units do not appear to be harmed as they would in a human.

Lastly, judged by human and other species clinical standards, a study with analyses of the giraffe's kidney function showed *all* clinical values to be within a *normal range; no signs of hypertension were found.* In those studies, standard clinical kidney function analyses included measurements of blood urea nitrogen (BUN); serum creatinine, plasma globulin, and plasma albumin.

So, the normal adult giraffe shows *no* signs of hypertension-related *disease* in its:

- heart or heart function (despite a thicker than average left heart wall)
- arteries or veins (no failure of the aorta or arteriosclerosis, especially)
- legs (no fluid build-up—edema)
- brain (no stroke)
- kidneys (no kidney failure)

Finally, to sum up: In addition to evolving long neck bones and coevolving a high blood pressure, the giraffe—in order to survive—would also have to coevolve every part of its cardiovascular system and every organ in its body to withstand the physical effects of its high blood pressure. And, once again, all such evolution/coevolution events would have to have come about *randomly*—non-linked, non-integrated, without purpose.

**The Giraffe's Neck.** We've seen that the giraffe needs a high blood pressure to move its blood up the six feet from its heart to its brain against the effects of gravity and that it suffers no consequences from its coevolved high blood pressure. But what happens to that same column of blood when the giraffe bends down to drink? Gravity causes the blood to rush to its head and the blood pressure in its head to *double*. Yet, the giraffe suffers no ill effects from that increase.

Damage to the brain from the doubled blood pressure is prevented by a sponge-like set of blood vessels called the *rete mirabile* at the base of the brain that expand, thus controlling the blood pressure actually entering the brain.

More remarkably, when the giraffe stands back up, it has a *unique* connection between two associated arteries feeding the brain (an anastomosis) that direct blood back into the brain rather than letting it drain away. To ensure the giraffe doesn't faint when it raises its head, the main veins draining the brain (jugular veins) also have "special valves [that] automatically close when the giraffe bends down and reopen when it [stands] back up."

Keep in mind that all these features had to have *randomly* coevolved for the giraffe to become the animal we see today. Randomly.

**The Giraffe's Challenge to Evolution.** When you look at the giraffe and its biology from even a high level as we just did, there is no question that it is an amazing mammal, both in terms of its anatomy and physiology, as well as its being a beautiful creature.

However, in terms of its proposed evolution, it has been estimated that for a short-necked giraffe ancestor to evolve anatomically and physiologically to our long-necked giraffe of today would literally require multiple tens of thousands of linked changes, and all would be contingent on random mutations. And those estimates do not appear to even begin to take into account the massive numbers of *additional* random mutations the giraffe's cardiovascular system would require to coevolve and keep pace with its lengthening neck.

Now, we need a brief but serious discussion about those required mutations. Early on, you found that the overriding key characteristic of genomic information is that it is stable when passed on from generation to generation. The biochemical machinery of the cell alone makes certain not only that "genetic homeostasis" is maintained, but that "genomic reorganizations" required for evolution are prevented.

However, you also know that when mutations *do* occur that are passed on, "they tend to disrupt function," that is, cause disease if the involved cell does not commit cell death (apoptosis). And as far as the speculated uncountable "positive" mutations needed for the giraffe to evolve is concerned, recall the mechanism proposed for the giraffe, that they *may* have come about as a result of "toxins that caused higher mutation rates and [therefore] a higher rate of evolution." But that explanation turns out to seem to have no basis in fact—a literature report explicitly states that neither toxins (chemical mutagens) nor ionizing radiation (a physical mutagen) are capable of causing genomic reorganizations (such as would be needed by the giraffe's ancestors). Because no source of genomic reorganization has been validated experimentally as producing a new animal, the ability or mutations to do so remains undocumented and pure speculation.

Another way of critically (and skeptically) looking at random mutations as the sole driving force for the evolution of the giraffe's neck, and therefore the coevolution of its other required anatomic and physiologic changes, is to ask direct questions challenging these evolutionary processes as science requires. Keep in mind, too, that any giraffe ancestors would not only have to have survived and thrived in their natural environment but also have made their way through the gateway of "Natural Selection" as the most fit. Such questions might include:

- **Number of mutations:** How many *random* mutations would it take to cause today's giraffe to evolve from a shorter necked ancestor? That estimate should include not only those mutations required for evolution of the giraffe's longer neck, but also the sum of those needed to coevolve all of the anatomic and physiological changes necessary to the cardiovascular system and all the organs it serves. The total anatomic changes alone have been estimated to involve some "25,000 protein-coding genes," affecting "200 joints, 300 bones associated with 1,000 ligaments and 4,000 tendons, 700 muscles," and on and on.

- **Sequence of mutations.** Recalling that no mutation could disrupt the physiological homeostasis of a giraffe ancestor (or it would likely die), what would be the *sequence* of random mutations required for the giraffe to evolve? That is—and keeping in mind all of the associated anatomic and physiologic changes needed (e.g., blood pressure)—in what order would the various systems have to evolve so that those changes would be accommodated by other systems without disrupting homeostasis?

- **Timeframe of changes.** Given that all evolutionary changes are *random,* and allowing for populations to grow, thrive, and evolve further, what would be a reasonable estimate of the timeframe involved for the modern giraffe to evolve?

- **Statistical odds.** Also, based on the foundation of *random* events required by evolution theory, and allowing for survival of various populations in the evolutionary tree of this animal, what are the estimated statistical odds of the giraffe evolving from a shorter necked ancestor? They would appear to be astronomical.

- **What is evolution's classification of the giraffe's evolution?** Finally, evolution of populations of organisms via Natural Selection can take one of two paths according to evolution theory models. Evolution can occur through "phyletic gradualism," in which populations undergo steady changes over an extended period of time, or they may exhibit no changes over long periods of time followed by rapid sets of changes, a model known as "punctuated equilibrium." Given the numerous unquestionably linked coevolution events the giraffe would have needed to become the animal it is from a short-necked ancestor, what evolution model does the giraffe's evolution correspond with? It would seem that *neither* applies.

These questions apply not only to the giraffe. Rather, they become a *universal framework* challenging evolutionary biology in any explanation of the evolution of *any* truly new animal from an ancestor—from jellyfish, to sharks, to dinosaurs, to mammals—to us.

## THE GIRAFFE AS *THE* PROTOTYPE EXAMPLE TO REJECT EVOLUTION

The biologic changes the giraffe would have had to endure to evolve from its proposed short-necked ancestor to the long-necked animal it is today are obviously a major issue. But, the complexity of the *process* required for the coevolution of its cardiovascular system to occur makes the evolution of its longer neck almost trivial.

The fallout of all of these combined issues is where random evolution collides headlong into the well-established, thoroughly documented and accepted physiologic principle of homeostasis.

**Why Couldn't The Giraffe Have Evolved?** The answer to that question is straightforward. All coevolution cardiovascular events needed by the giraffe would have to have happened not only in sets, but *simultaneously* with the giraffe's lengthening neck at any step to maintain the physiological integrity and homeostasis of the animal. In biologic actuality, they would have had to be, in effect, evolutionarily coordinated. This integrated process is the *only* way the giraffe could have maintained its internal physiological stability.

But the requirement for an integrated process conflicts in *every* respect with *the* core principle, *the* foundation of evolution: that *all* events have to occur without purpose, that is, randomly—no one event can ever depend on or be linked with any other in terms of timing or effect. Taken together, and based on established science, you have an impossible biologic situation that gets even more impossible when applied to major groups of new animals ever evolving.

Take, for example, the claimed evolution of mammals from reptiles.

In considering this evolutionary change, once again, Dr. Stephen Meyer's axiom directly applies here: "where *did* [all] *the* [new genetic] *information come from to build all these new proteins, cells and body parts?*"

It applies because tissue, protein, and enzyme function depend *directly* on the temperature of their environment.

Let me explain.

The biological evolutionary and coevolutionary changes needed for reptiles to evolve to mammals are simply incomprehensible just in terms of the issue of their core body temperatures. Core body temperature in turn affects every protein, enzyme, and tissue, because their function (especially enzymes) depends *directly* on the temperature of their environment. Recall that reptiles are technically *poikilotherms*; that is, they have no metabolic mechanism to control their internal, core temperatures, which as a result, are variable (within limits). Rather, they depend entirely on using their environment to maintain their body temperatures, even though some may have muscle mass to produce heat (i.e., endothermic properties). As a result, reptilian proteins operate well over a relatively broad range of temperatures.

In sharp contrast, mammals are *homeothermic*, that is, they have relatively constant core temperatures which they metabolically and physiologically control. They do not depend on their environment to maintain their body temperature. Further, mammalian proteins have a very sharp optimum temperature peak well above those of reptiles.

What all of this means in terms of the speculated reptile to mammal evolution is that *every* reptilian protein would have to be "remade" not only for mammals in general to evolve, but *specifically* for each mammal, because all have unique core temperatures. Where did all of this genetic information come from? Given the giraffe's biological impossibility of evolving from short-necked ancestors and at the same time maintaining homeostasis, such requirements point to the utter impossibility of any form of such random evolution ever occurring.

Rather, it points directly toward Creation, and in particular, a Creator's Intelligent Design.

**The Giraffe Rejects Evolution.** Earlier, we talked about an absolute standard of the scientific method: that to validate a proposed theory required direct, demonstrated, and confirmed evidence. And as Dr. Feynman pointed out, fulfilling that standard can only be done through "experiment."

So, could our analysis of what we know about evolution of the giraffe's neck and blood pressure be considered as an experiment or not? No, at least not in the very restricted sense of the word, because we had no specific experimental design to test against a hypothesis or theory under controlled conditions in a laboratory for which we did not know the answer. But, the giraffe clearly *does* serve as an observational study type experiment in which we compared its biology against the underlying theory of evolution: that this animal evolved through random mutations of its ancestors.

In that respect, the coevolution of every specific cardiovascular change required by the giraffe's step-wise lengthening neck would be a *predictable* consequence, the critical element of any experiment. And, because such changes would be predictable and have been found, doesn't that result fulfill the standards of the scientific method and validate evolution? Evolution biology would certainly say so.

However, the true answer is unequivocally no, it would not, not in the least, and why? Because evolution has not only ignored but has utterly failed to predict and then demonstrate *how* homeostasis could be maintained throughout all the biological changes that would have to take place during the giraffe's evolution.

As a result, evolution as an explanation for how all life came to be *cannot* be considered science or fact. Random events *cannot* maintain homeostasis as a result of the multiple events that would be needed during the evolution of any truly new animal; in fact, as the giraffe so well illustrates, it would be a biologic impossibility. And without homeostasis, life could not exist.

So, the giraffe gives us an experiment with which to reject the whole of evolution. But what about all the fossil evidence and similarities in DNA that evolution claims? Doesn't the vast sum of that evidence validate evolution?

Einstein would likely not agree, not in light of the giraffe.

Recall his famous insight (my emphasis):

"No amount of experimentation can ever prove me right; *a single experiment can prove me wrong.*"

" . . . a single experiment." In the case of evolution, that one experiment is the giraffe.

# CHAPTER 8

# EVOLUTION'S IMPOSSIBLE CHALLENGES

We have just reviewed the impossible biology required to support evolution of the giraffe. That situation raises the question: What evidence—that is clear, convincing, and beyond dispute—*does* evolution have to support its claim that evolution is science and fact?

All evidence claimed to support random evolution apart from God is good *only as long as you fully accept and do not question* that it is true in the first place. Once you've crossed that bridge and do not return, everything evolution asserts to be true makes sense. It is as though once you hold evolution to be true, you can then reason backward to make the evolution of every natural creature "fit" your theory.

As we just saw with the example of the giraffe, however, evolution does *not* take into account the physiological principle of homeostasis. In fact, evolution devoid of God and based strictly on random events is irreconcilable with maintaining an animal's homeostasis.

As I'm sure you are aware, evolution itself is built principally on two lines of evidence, one well documented and one questionable. The first consists of fossils of increasingly complex organisms appearing over time and similarities in the DNA of closely related organisms—if DNAs are similar, then surely the organisms must have evolved from a common ancestor. The more questionable line of evidence concerns the issue of homologies: how animals seem to have similar features across major groups, such as finding flippers in fish, sea turtles (reptiles) and whales (mammals).

However, note that neither type of evidence evolution presents is *direct* evidence founded on any experimental documentation to provide "evidence that is so clear, so tangible, so convincing that it does *not* require any reasoning process." Rather, both are entirely circumstantial and can only be concluded as true through interpretation and inference (i.e., human reasoning subject to bias). Further, this limitation means that any conclusions evolution draws can only be made authoritative through nonscientific techniques (e.g., "scientific consensus") to show that evolution is "truth," that it is "fact." But that approach is *not* valid. Evolution *cannot* assert itself to be true and accepted on anyone's or any group's "say so" without sufficient supporting experimental evidence. In these regards, *evolution is consistent with the characteristics of a pseudoscience.*

Finally, evolution utterly fails entirely to disclose the crippling limitations of such reasoning. These and their significance are *never acknowledged or plainly stated as such* by evolution proponents, as required by good science practice.

## THE FAILURE OF EVOLUTION'S EVIDENCE

So, evolution is built entirely on inference and reasoning without direct evidence, but how does such reasoning work? You've already read that in the case of DNA, known similarities between DNAs of various obviously related animals are interpreted (through inference) to claim that they all came from a common ancestor. Again note that there is no experimental documentation to support this assumption.

In the case of new animals evolving from existing ones, inference is used to link—correlate—the sequence of fossils increasing in complexity over hundreds of millions of years of time in order to conclude that the speculated *process* that made them—evolution—is true. In doing so, evolution *makes an assumption without being able to directly demonstrate that the process is, in fact, true.* In science, correlating a possible sequence with an observation in this manner is *not* definitive or the final word. In short, "correlation is *not* causation." Making an assumption in this manner is a major error in logic, formally known as a *post hoc* type error and does *not* validate evolution as fact.

What about evolution's claim that hundreds of millions, if not billions, of years were needed for the life we see today to come about? Is that estimate of the earth's age reasonable? Dr. Don DeYoung and his colleagues would say unequivocally no. This research group conducted what is known as the RATE (Radioisotopes and the Age of The Earth) study. Their work updated the standard method of how the earth's age is calculated according to the decay of radioisotopes (radiometric dating) that yields the earth's age at billions of years. To conduct the RATE study, they closely examined different interpretations of radioisotope dating of the geologic record. Their results were truly significant and unexpected, because they provided an estimate that the earth's age is *only about 6,000 years old*. Thus, science appears to confirm the Earth's age as it is calculated from the Bible.

Moreover, in the past ten years or so, at least three dinosaur fossils (a *Triceratops*, a *hadrosaur*, and a *T. rex*) have been discovered in which soft tissue, including blood cells, have been found. Such soft tissue could never have lasted the millions of years evolution claims. Based on those findings in the case of *Triceratops* soft tissue, its age was estimated to be on the order of only 4,000 years old, a startling finding that was published in two scientific journals.

The importance and fallout of the *Triceratops* findings will be discussed in Chapter 9.

## EVOLUTION CLAIMS TO BE SCIENCE

Creation is sometimes known to evolutionary biology as "special creation" in which every living organism was specifically created by God. As such, it is claimed by evolution not to be science because it requires faith that cannot be demonstrated by the scientific method. However, the same evolutionary biology holds that evolution is science, a position that both the AAAS and the National Association of Biology Teachers hold, see Chapter 9, "Is Evolution a Dogma?". Herein lies a problem for evolution without solution or possible explanation. First, note how Creation ("special creation") is viewed by evolution in this comment from an evolutionary biology textbook: "The hypothesis of special creation cannot be tested [tested how? By experiment?] and so is not considered to be scientific." But at the same time, note that this same textbook states that because evolution is a "well-supported" theory (supported how?) that has "survived many different tests (*none* dealing with actual biology yielding direct evidence, only from inference of observations)," and as such, *laboratory experiments are not necessarily required.*

So—how can evolution claim that it meets the rigorous standards of science that require direct evidence from testing (i.e., experiments) but then state that such testing is "not necessarily required" in its case? In doing that, evolution thereby exempts and excuses itself from the basic standards of the scientific method. In that regard, recall the characteristics of a pseudoscience you read earlier, namely that it:

- attempts to present itself as science, *but*

- does *not* adhere to the rigorous standards of the scientific method in how it is performed, *or*

- simply *cannot* be performed by the scientific method; specifically, that it . . .

- proposes hypotheses that *cannot* be shown to be wrong through data obtained by direct experiment or observational studies, *and*

- uses euphemisms, vague or ambiguous phrasing, and wording that means whatever the individual wants it to mean, and *finally*

- presents detailed evidence only consistent with its conclusions but that utterly fails to *carefully* explore (omits) evidence that is *not* consistent with them

Now ask yourself: How many of these criteria could be applied to evolution, the question being, is evolution a science or not? Would it be more appropriate to classify it as a pseudoscience?

Moreover, if in the case of abiogenesis and evolution of new animals from pre-existing ones, it justifies itself as truth only through inference and indirect evidence, then what about the excellent work of Drs. Stephen Meyer and Michael Behe on Intelligent Design and Irreducible Complexity, which draws conclusions in exactly the same manner and with far more compelling evidence? Evolution will not allow any discussion or consideration of that similarity.

## THE BOTTOM LINE FOR EVOLUTION

Evolution, in effect, appears to want to "have its cake and eat it too." In other words, evolution hypocritically wants to hold Creation to strict science standards that it itself does not abide by, justifying its position by asserting that "laboratory experiments are not necessarily required." Sorry, but for evolution in the most strict sense of the term (new, unique, never-been-seen-before animals arising from existing ones) to then claim that it is "science" and "fact" when 1) it uses inference exclusively to draw what appear to be conclusions not open to challenge, and 2) it has *no* direct evidence and cannot develop any to demonstrate that new animals arise from existing ones, that claim just doesn't wash; in fact, it is bogus and a "red herring." What direct evidence evolutionary biology does offer, like the soapberry bug, clearly demonstrates adaptation of an organism to its environment based on pre-existing—not new—genetic information. That is *not* evolution.

What, then, is the essential difference between evolution and Creation? The only way that evolution can assert itself to be science, truth, and fact is through secular inference and reasoning; it *cannot* validate itself as a natural science that requires direct evidence from experiment. For evolution to acclaim that reasoning—something focused on and constructed solely by *human* effort—can explain the origin of literally all life we see and know is in essence to arrogantly exult and glorify itself, to deify itself.

How does God view such a human effort? Here is what He says through the prophet Isaiah (Is. 5:21):

> "Woe to those who are wise in their own eyes and clever in their own sight."

# CHAPTER 9

# NULLIFYING GOD: EVOLUTION'S END GAME

*"When men choose not to believe in God, they do not thereafter believe in nothing, they then become capable of believing in anything."*

Theologian G.K. Chesterton (1874–1936)

When I first approached and researched evolution as a science, the information I found in academic evolution textbooks, as extensive as it was, didn't seem quite right. I eventually came to realize that the conflict between evolution and Creation had nothing to do with the principles of science. Instead, evolution was misusing the neutral tool of science in a spiritual battle against Creation.

As an agnostic, Charles Darwin wanted to use science to show that everything appearing to have purpose—all life—in fact actually had none, that it was all due to random events being "sifted by the blind, automatic forces of natural selection." Darwin used these principles in his 1859 classic *Origin of the Species,* which set forth a "scientific" basis for how every living organism came to be. Moreover, it was consistent with a growing rationalist movement of that era, secularism, a movement dedicated to nullify God. Today, the two work together to attempt to achieve that end.

To understand how this condition might come about, we first need to understand what secularism is, how it uses evolution to attempt to establish itself in our culture today, and then how it is being used to nullify God.

## SECULARISM

Secularism elevates human reasoning and experience to the highest level of authority and learning conceivable, and restricts knowledge to those areas that could be only "tested by the experience of this life," a criterion that fit well with but misused the experimental approach applied by science. The focus of this movement remains to actively eliminate *any* mention of Christianity from the public arena, and it has *absolute* separation of church and state as its primary objective.

This movement formally bore its "fruit" in 1885 when the American Secular Union (ASU) was formed, with numerous "free-thinker" organizations subsequently developing over the years. Consistent with the principles of secularism, the ASU dismissed anything having to do with God and Christianity, instead extolling human reason above all else.

At that time, the ASU set forth a list of nine demands. Among others, these in essence required that *no* public official would be able to openly mention or refer to God at *any* time under *any* conditions (even in the taking of oaths), nor would any special consideration be given to churches in terms of their operation (e.g., they would not be exempt from taxes). Prominent in secularism's goals, it would effectively *forbid* public teaching of Creation, because it demanded that "the use of the Bible for religious purposes in public schools [e.g., to present Creation] shall be *prohibited.*"

Today, most of these objectives have been achieved in the United States through court rulings. Secularism is considered established and defended by evolution proponents, and our people suffer for it.

**Secularism, Creation, and Evolution.** Because it has an absolute reliance on and exults human reason to be able—by experience—to explain everything we can see, know, and touch as its foundation, secularism offers a godless vision of the universe and life. In this vision, everything comes to exist exclusively through the process of random natural events that have no purpose, consistent with Darwin's viewpoint.

To explore these relationships, we begin with astrophysicist Dr. Carl Sagan, who helped write and was host of the former PBS series, *The Cosmos*, first broadcast in 1980. He did not classify himself as an atheist, but rather as one who believed that only the evidence provided by science had all the answers to our existence. In that manner, he rejected even the *possibility* of Creation in favor of human reason. Note how he wove that perspective into each episode of *The Cosmos* as he opened it with the following statement:

"The Cosmos is all that is, or was, or ever will be."

When Dr. Sagan asserts, *"all* that is" (i.e., the present), *"ever* was" (i.e., the past), and "or *ever* will be" (i.e., the future), stop and reflect on exactly what he is saying. There is no question that God is not only *not* part of this picture but that it meshes perfectly with the tenets of secularism. Also, isn't it interesting how this declaration of secularism as the *only* truth is actually a counterfeit of Scripture? Note how it misleadingly parallels what God emphasizes to us throughout Scripture, especially as Jesus glorifies Himself in the Book of Revelation (Rev. 1:8, ESV):

"I am the Alpha and Omega," says the Lord God, "who is and who was and who is to come, the Almighty."

What is Jesus telling us here? He declares *Himself* to be sovereign, the Lord of all—"the past, present, and future."

Without knowing what Scripture tells us, the potential of Dr. Sagan's statement to deceive and lull the unsuspecting into disbelief is powerful and amazing (see John 8:44). Moreover, it is absolutely consistent with a view that evolution is secularism's counterfeit for Creation (2 Cor. 11:14–15).

Clearly, Dr. Sagan's statement explicitly proclaims a dogma of secularism as far as the universe is concerned. But in that regard, note how it *also* essentially canonizes evolution's complete reliance on a secular, natural explanation for all life in every way. What Dr. Sagan tells us is that God is not only not needed to explain the universe and Creation, He just doesn't exist, and science should be exalted for leading us to the truth in His place.

Does secularism carry over from Creation into how all life came to be, that is, abiogenesis and evolution? To answer that question, witness what evolutionary biologist and Professor of Psychology, Dr. David P. Barash of Washington State University, had to say. In his article "God, Darwin, and My Biology Class," Dr. Barash states the following:

> "Since Darwin . . . we have come to understand that an entirely natural and undirected process, namely random variation plus natural selection, contains all that is needed to generate extraordinary levels of nonrandomness."

No question that Dr. Barash's statement, typical of much evolution text and science writing, is somewhat dense, convoluted, and confusing at first. However, notice the essence of what he is claiming when he talks about "extraordinary levels of nonrandomness." This cumbersome description fits what we call *all created life*, in all its splendor and diversity.

Translated, what Dr. Barash is saying is that all life we see and know is due entirely to random events—purposeless randomness generates purposefulness as evidenced by life, an absolutely preposterous, pretzel-like piece of logic. Nonetheless, Dr. Barash asserts this position, through which he utterly dismisses even the remote possibility of a Creator. As to his own personal perspective, Dr. Barash was described as an "unapologetic atheist," among other things in a 2013 interview.

The critical point Dr. Barash misses (as well as most others who hold this position) is that what he proclaims *absolutely* depends on abiogenesis being documented to be fact, and it is not. Simply accepting it as true for whatever reason without providing required supporting evidence *is not science*. In fact, recall that it is one of the many logical fallacies used to uphold evolution, in this case one called the argument from ignorance, which occurs when someone essentially claims,

"Well, we know [something] is true, because even without the evidence, what else could it be?" The answer is that without specific, conclusive evidence beyond dispute, the explanation is entirely speculation.

We will return to Dr. Barash's position shortly.

**Not All Scientists Who Support Evolution Are Secularists.** Some who support evolution clearly see God's hand as guiding evolution. For example, Dr. Francis Collins, head of the Human Genome Project at the National Institutes of Health, makes a case for "theistic evolution," that is, evolution guided by God.

Note too Dr. Thomas Dobzhansky (1900–1975), a Ukrainian geneticist, whom evolution proponents routinely quote as having said,

"Nothing in biology makes sense except in the light of evolution."

And, Dr. Dobzhansky did indeed say that. However, what evolution proponents ignore is that Dr. Dobzhansky was *not* arguing for an evolution devoid of God; he was an orthodox Christian, although some considered him to be a pantheist. Rather, he could apparently not accept special Creation, that God had specifically made each and every species. For him, God had to have caused evolution to happen over hundreds of millions of years of time.

**Does Secular Science's Position on Evolution Tarnish Its General Use?** Emphatically, no! Let there be no question that it does not. Science is perhaps the ultimate tool, when it is properly applied, for the purpose it was developed: to find what is true and real about the natural world. However, never forget for a moment that it is *only* a tool, and that it is used by fallible human beings who may have preconceptions, biases, and agendas. World-renown climatologist Dr. Roy Spencer (University of Alabama, Huntsville) summed up this characteristic so well when he said (my emphasis):

" . . . the existence of bias in scientific research . . . is *always* present."

So, although some might "pooh-pooh" this fact, there is little question that human bias is *always* involved in science (and every other *human* endeavor) to some extent, as Dr. Spencer confirmed. What does that reality imply? For perspective, reflect on Scottish evangelist Oswald Chambers' (1874–1917) insight, then apply his thought to how evolution presents itself as science and fact. He said,

> "Every art, every healing, every good can be used for an opposite purpose."

In other words, something as simple as fire can be used for good (e.g., for warmth, cooking) or destructive purposes (e.g., arson).

The tool of science is no exception to this rule. To those successful in working with it, it can bring prestige and a wonderful sense of accomplishment. But at the same time, it can cause an exaggerated sense of self-importance to develop that can corrupt and make the practitioner serve it, rather than the other way around.

## IS EVOLUTION A DOGMA?

Many have described evolution as a dogma, but evolution is adamant that it is not. So, is it or isn't it? Before answering this question, we need to talk briefly about what the essence of dogma is so there is no misunderstanding.

**What Is a Dogma?** Theological discussions of dogma can be extensive and complex, but at least three basic points stand out that characterize dogma as the term is commonly used. Specifically, a dogma is:

- religious in nature
- not only a truth concerning faith or morals,
- but an *immutable* truth, because it has been revealed by God

And, if a truth has been revealed by God, you can trust it completely, because "it is impossible for God to lie" (Heb. 6:18).

Characterized in this manner, the term *dogma* doesn't sound like it has much, if anything, in common with secular evolution, does it? As a matter of fact, it sounds as though dogma is about as far removed from evolution as "the east is from west" (Ps. 103:12). With evolution being entirely secular and having nothing to do with God, it cannot be even remotely religious in nature, and it is certainly not a revealed religious truth.

Further, it rather forcefully ignores, dismisses, and rejects any possibility that God (or even a "god") might have had anything to do with life or Creation at all, because, in the case of Intelligent Design at least, Creation was found by a court to be "a religious concept, not science."

And if a religious concept, it must therefore be based on faith. And faith, atheist Richard Dawkins tells us, "is the great cop-out, the great excuse to evade the need to think and evaluate evidence." In the case of evolution, Dawkins' statement implies that science gives us all the evidence we need to make the correct decision; our error is that we simply haven't thought about or evaluated it as we should.

However, in taking this position, evolution is in essence deifying science in its explanation for life in that it is:

- *absolute* in proclaiming random, natural evolution as fact
- *adamant* that religious Creation not be seriously considered under any conditions

Thus, the manner in which evolution is proclaimed by its proponents—that is, that it is a fact beyond all reasonable doubt—bypasses the skepticism that science requires. It thereby becomes the equivalent of an absolute and unquestionable fact. In doing so, its proponents defy such scientists as Einstein, who acknowledged his limitations and uncertainties when he essentially admitted that there could be one more thing he did not know. Recall his humility when he said, "A *single* experiment can prove me wrong."

By taking this absolute position and rejecting any skepticism, evolution holds itself to be an immutable truth. In doing so, it becomes the secular equivalent of a dogma. And because of its nature, a dogma, when it is misused, can easily become authoritarian—no dissent allowed. History shows us time and again that those who misuse dogma can—and do—regulate, dictate, and mandate whatever they want to achieve and in doing so, take the position of demagogues.

**How Is the Dogma of Evolution Presented to Our Society?** Before we begin this particular journey, it might be useful to quickly think back to claims made for evolution by its supporters, who, in essence, assert that "The science is settled; evolution is real and fact." Statements made by Richard Dawkins, Bill Nye ("the science guy") who wrote *Undeniable* (St. Martin's Griffin, 2015), Dr. David P. Barash, and many others leave little doubt on this point.

Recall, too, how evolution is supported by a premier science organization, the American Association for the Advancement of Science (AAAS), considered "the world's largest scientific society." In addition to stating unequivocally that evolution is "one of the most robust and widely accepted principles of modern science," it further states that "there is no more scientific justification for criticizing evolution than other scientific theories . . . " (e.g., "the theory of gravity" among others). Such authoritative statements tell us that even questioning the basis of evolution is no longer warranted or considered appropriate by evolution opponents, again consistent with the essential characteristics of a dogma.

Given the public positions of such prominent supporters and science organizations, it should be no surprise that teaching any form of Creation in public schools is not only actively discouraged, it is simply proscribed, consistent with the demands of secularism. For example, the National Association of Biology Teachers (NABT) cautions that, "Science teachers must reject calls" to teach "non-naturalistic or supernatural" explanations for life, because "they are outside of the scope of science," and "do not conform to [fundamental] scientific standards." In short, Creation should not be taught because it is not science but is rather a "supernatural" explanation. The NABT statement is endorsed by The Society for the Study of Evolution. Note, however, that the NABT does not acknowledge or allude to the glaring limitations we have found evolution involves.

Further, the AAAS also takes that same position by stating that the teaching of Intelligent Design "does not belong in the science classroom." The reason? Intelligent Design depends on a "supernatural designer," and therefore becomes a "religious concept." Again, because Creation becomes a religious "concept" and is not science, therefore all who take that position wrongly hold the tool of science higher than God. As with the NABT, the AAAS does not acknowledge or allude to the absolute limitations of evolution evidence and theory.

However, some position papers on teaching evolution take these relatively neutral prohibitions a significant step further by implementing certain demands proposed in 1885 by the ASU. Consider, for example, The Center for Inquiry Office of Public Policy's position concerning teaching of Intelligent Design (2007). This organization goes so far as to tell us that creationists have an "anti-science and"— note carefully the next term—"*anti-secularism* agenda" in attempting to have Intelligent Design presented as an alternative to evolution in public schools. This same paper also notes that public schools are the "largest public institution in the *first secular democracy in history*," and emphasizes the "separation of church and state" throughout it as well.

Consistent with evolution holding to the principles of secularism, those advocating it apparently think there's the potential for great harm in the teaching of Creation. So, from their point of view, not only would Creation confront the limitations of evolution, but in doing so, it would challenge and threaten their entire belief system. For example, in a 2012 article from the *Los Angeles Times*, "Does creationism have a place at a public school?" retiring biology teacher Tom Philips is said to be "disturbed" when students turn in reports that question the "irrefutable evidence" that Darwin was right. Moreover, Mr. Phillips also feels that the teaching of Creation is actually an attempt to "*indoctrinate* [the students] with something that's not true."

Mr. Phillips' position is an ironic but not unexpected one. Why? If the students are not allowed to be presented with an alternative explanation for life, then they *in fact* are actually being indoctrinated *with evolution—and secularism.* Such a position is reminiscent of Paul's statement in Romans 2:1. "You, therefore, have no excuse, you who pass judgment on someone else, for at whatever point you judge another, you are condemning yourself, because you who pass judgment *do the same things*" (emphasis mine).

But Mr. Philips is not alone in his concern. Witness at the least what evolution proponent Bill Nye ("The Science Guy") has to say on this point.

In a 2012 ABC television interview called "Bill Nye 'The Science Guy' Hits Evolution Deniers," Mr. Nye equates "denial" of evolution with "*harm* to young people," because they are *not* learning science. Further, he then urges adults to support young people being taught evolution:

> "And I say to the grownups, if you want to deny evolution and live in your world, in your world that's completely inconsistent with everything we observe in the universe, that's fine, but don't make your kids do it because we need them."

What Mr. Nye is effectively saying is that science—a useful but inanimate, lifeless tool originating from human reasoning, *not* Creation or faith that comes from God—is our *only* way to understand life. In this, he is taking a position fully in line with secularism. Moreover, Mr. Nye also asserts that Creation is "inconsistent with everything we [see] in the universe," implying that *only* evolution *is* consistent. In taking this position, Mr. Nye is essentially and wrongly deifying science as others have done who advocate evolution. In that view, faith is unnecessary and, consistent with Richard Dawkins who said that it "is the great cop-out," it would only get in our way of properly understanding the "evidence" presented to us by science.

But beyond that, notice that Mr. Nye also indirectly affirms the *certainty* of evolution when he emphasizes its denial ("denial of evolution"; "deny evolution") by Creation supporters. He clearly believes that evolution is absolute fact. His position in this interview is not a surprise. Rather it is completely consistent with the one he takes in his book, *Undeniable,* when he said, "What would the *deniers* have us do?" In other words, Mr. Nye is calling Creation supporters "evolution deniers," an *ad hominem,* which brings up an interesting point as a result.

Why use an *ad hominem* if the evidence and rationale for evolution were unquestionably true, if it were an "incontrovertible" fact supported by "irrefutable evidence"? Such characterization would be totally unnecessary. Recall what an *ad hominem* is, because it has nothing to do with science—it is a debate technique characterized by abusive name calling with the intent to silence or intimidate. The *ad hominem* is used by a debater to attempt to win an otherwise *unwinnable* argument. Its use in the case of evolution again emphasizes that supporters want *no* dissention or counterargument to get in their way of instituting evolution as the standard for how life and all its diversity came to be.

These brief examples are clear: Any attempt to present Creation as an explanation for life is not welcome in the public arena, and it must be actively stamped out. Evolution proponents appear to hold that only science has a place to explain life, an extreme position consistent with secularism and today known as "scientism" (see Appendix I). Sad. But, this stand does not appear to be accidental . . .

Why is there this need to exalt human intelligence as the "be all and end all"?

## EVOLUTION AND OUR CULTURE

How is evolution affecting our culture? Dr. Barash's statement we saw earlier is a crystal-clear example that perfectly reflects the ideology of secular naturalism that evolution is pushing us toward. Recall how Dr. Barash asserted that "random variation" leads to "extraordinary levels of nonrandomness" (what we call *created life*). The bottom line of this approach is to show that God is *not* needed to explain life, and that position is what is being taught.

Moreover, the position paper of the National Association for Biology Teachers and the Position Paper from The Center for Inquiry Office of Public Policy (as well as others) strictly hold that only science is needed to explain all life, from its origin to what we see today. The "supernatural" (i.e., God) is unnecessary and excluded.

Thus, for those who hold to this position, it seems that God can be actively relegated to a distant myth. He becomes an explanation of the ancients disproved and debunked by modern science. As such, teaching of biblical Creation becomes "anti-science," as well as anti-secular, and it should neither be taught nor mentioned in school in their view. Witness this article that appeared online as just one example: "White House Petition to Ban Creationism Gathering Steam." That 2013 petition, to ban the teaching of Creationism and Intelligent Design in public schools, gathered almost 24,000 signatures in the first week.

The question once again is this: Why is there this unstinting, absolute resistance to teaching evolution? Ken Ham, president of Answers in Genesis, deals with this question directly in the same article:

> "This anti-creationist petition is yet another example of the intolerance of evolutionist activists who do not want to see any challenge to their deeply held secularist worldview . . . "

Mr. Ham's comment raises the key question: What evidence is there that those who are "anti-Creation" do not want to be challenged?

First, briefly recall the adamant positions held by those who support evolution, such as Mr. Bill Nye, the NABT, The Center for Inquiry Office of Public Policy, and professional science organizations (e.g., the AAAS). But then, there are other, more direct examples as well, two of which are offered below.

**Example 1.** In the January 16, 2016 issue of the science journal *PLoS ONE*, scientists Ming-Jin Liu and his colleagues published the article, "Biomechanical Characteristics of Hand Coordination in Grasping Activities of Daily Living," the title of which seems innocent enough, as was the well-written article. Innocent, that is, until the authors included this single comment in the article's abstract and as a conclusion, when they said that the mechanical architecture of the human hand *"is the proper design by the Creator."* Not "a" Creator, but *"the"* Creator, the word "Creator" being capitalized in the article.

When it was discovered, that statement set off the equivalent of a reactive firestorm, in which *PLoS ONE* editors issued an apology to their readers, the article was retracted, and one editor is said to have commented, "I feel outraged by the publication of a [manuscript] making explicit reference to creationism." Another incensed editor said, "As an editor of *PLoS ONE*, I am ashamed this ever got to be published, and I am ready to resign if this is not retracted immediately," and like comments followed from there.

Science requires reasoned debate and discussion of concepts and data to try to arrive at a truth of the natural world. This example highlights how the "science" of evolution may trash that requirement when Creation is involved.

**Example 2.** The dinosaur *Triceratops* with its three horns is unique and instantly recognizable to anyone who has once seen its skeleton or a full-sized model of it. These large animals (about 24-27 feet long and 6 feet in height) are alleged to have roamed the earth about 68 million years ago. Until biologist Mark Armitage (California State University, Northridge) came along, that is.

Armitage was on a fossil dig at a famous site in Montana in 2012 and had discovered the largest *Triceratops* horn yet observed. Given the supposed age of *Triceratops*, imagine then his surprise when he found soft (non-bony) tissue in the *Triceratops* fossil horn he had unearthed and taken back to his laboratory. Not just soft tissue, but *cells within the soft tissue* of the bones (bone-degrading osteocytes) when he examined the tissue under a microscope. With that find, he argued that if the fossil were actually millions of years old, such cells would have long since decayed.

Based on these findings, published in peer-reviewed science journals in November 2012 and February 2013, Armitage estimated the *Triceratops* to be *only* about *4,000 years old* at the most, an age fully consistent with the age of the earth as recorded in Genesis. This finding did not sit well with one university official who is reported to have "stormed" into Armitage's office in June 2012 shouting, "We are not going to tolerate your religion in this department!" Armitage was further able to conclude in a lawsuit filed for him that "these dinosaurs roamed the planet relatively recently."

Note, however, that Mr. Armitage's findings are completely consistent with, and independently confirm, those of the RATE (Radioisotopes and the Age of The Earth) study by Dr. Don DeYoung and colleagues, mentioned earlier, which estimated the earth's age at about 6,000 years.

But why the lawsuit? Armitage was subsequently fired from his position after publication of his articles. His lawsuit charged religious discrimination and further stated that what happened to him was "an attempt to silence scientific speech at a public university." At that time, the university simply noted that he had been only a temporary employee—after 38 months on the job and over 30 previous publications to his credit.

So once again, we have another example of how the "science" of evolution dismisses reasoned debate and discussion when Creation as revealed in the Bible is involved. Rather, the end game becomes more clear: Dissent is *not* allowed.

These two examples, coupled with the other evidence we've covered so far, strongly suggest that those who advocate for evolution advocate for *the* position of control. As such, they are accorded the decision-making power by their colleagues to block publications and dismiss any dissenting information or opinions. Does evolution actually press on strongly? Not only is no other conclusion possible, but there is no evidence to the contrary.

Why? The only possible explanation that ties all this evidence together is that there is an underlying agenda. In which case, the only reasonable question that can answer that "why" is this: What is the end game of evolution?

## EVOLUTION'S END GAME

Now we are in a position to legitimately ask the question: What is the end game of evolution? Although secularism claims to elevate human experience, learned moral behavior, and intellectual capacity to the "highest possible level . . . [which shows] the practical sufficiency of natural morality apart from . . . the Bible," this human-centered movement is *not* the intentional end game of evolution.

In fact, many (not all) of those who are evolution proponents might be surprised to even find they are on a parallel path with secularism. If asked, they would likely take a neutral academic stance and consider evolution to be only "evolution," and science to be only "science." But evolution and secularism share at least one key characteristic in common.

To find out what that might be, let's first consider this incredible insight from Oswald Chambers in his inspirational book, *My Utmost For His Highest* that applies directly to evolution. In his July 18 devotion, *The Mystery of Believing*, he points out that:

> "There is nothing miraculous about the things we can explain. We [intellectually] command what we are able to explain, consequently, it is natural to seek to explain."

In this statement, look closely at where Chambers correctly focuses his emphasis: Consistent with secularism, it is on the supremacy of the *self*, and it shines light especially on the self apart from Christ that is still enslaved to sin. Notice in particular the word "we," especially when he points out that, *"we command."* We command—not anyone else, and in that manner, we express the hidden need to be in control, to be unchallenged as our own gods, whether we realize it or not.

And how does this all come to be in the natural world? If *"we"* can explain some seeming miraculous event as natural, then Chambers says that because *"we"* [intellectually] own it, *"we"* command it, and *"we"* are in charge, in control, it is "natural [for us] to seek to explain."

Now, apply that thinking to evolution: if *we* can explain how all life came to be in terms of random nature—apart from God—how all life is nothing miraculous in the least, then what do we need God for? And if we choose not to believe because we think we have been able to explain the miraculous event as natural, then recall theologian G. K. Chesterton's simple but incredible insight:

> "When men choose not to believe in God, they do not thereafter believe in nothing, they then become capable of believing in anything."

"They then become capable of believing in anything." Anything! That seeming ability to make oneself an idol independent of God, making one's life choices without being accountable to anyone, is a very powerful and addicting temptation. And, that being the case, we can now begin to understand why evolution persists in proclaiming itself as "truth," even though it has no direct evidence for doing so. In a nutshell, making the "self" supreme appears to be *exactly* the unacknowledged, hidden, even covert goal of evolution. But, why should this be? Recall what Paul warned us about in his letter to the Ephesians for direction:

> "For our struggle is not against flesh and blood, but against the rulers, against the authorities, against the powers of this dark world and against the spiritual forces of evil in the heavenly realms" (Eph. 6:12).

But is evolution in effect pushing us to become independent of God? The answer is an unequivocal "yes." Keep in mind what evolution is stridently proclaiming—that if it is true, that if it is "fact," that if it has "proved" that all life came from *random* events, then it is telling us that *God is not needed.* It's as simple as that.

For an absolutely clear example of how this thinking works, let's go back to Dr. Barash, an "unapologetic atheist." Recall the substance of what he teaches as applied to evolution—namely, as complex and unique as we humans and all life *seems* to be, we are simply the result of "an entirely natural and undirected [i.e., random] process," that results in "extraordinary levels of nonrandomness."

Although Dr. Barash's assertion makes no logical sense at all (randomness results in nonrandomness?), the substance of what he is saying is that because *we* can explain life through evolution, then there's *nothing* miraculous here! Note that Dr. Barash's position is a perfect example from today that exactly echoes Oswald Chambers' incredible insight of over 100 years ago, that there is not only "nothing miraculous about things we can explain," but that we "command" them. In stark contrast, we certainly cannot command God, who is a mystery.

As I confessed to you earlier, I was once among those who unquestioningly accepted evolution for most of my life, never critically thinking about it. It was science, after all . . . until God opened my eyes to the actual truth. And, from my three decades of professional laboratory science experience with other colleagues in applied biology, and from the evidence I obtained in researching the materials for this book, I can assure you that Dr. Barash is far from alone in his thinking.

As I'm sure you can imagine, the outcome of rejecting God can and will get worse, much worse, because in *choosing* not to believe in God, men "become capable of believing in anything." So, if evolution were to have truly taken care of God once and for all, then what?

Professor of Bioethics Peter Singer, who presently holds an endowed chair at Princeton University, is a clear example of what the goal of evolution can yield. Prof. Singer is reported to have argued that "Darwinism logically entails a rejection of the Judeo-Christian sanctity-of-life ethic." And, given Darwin's push to proclaim all life purposeless and simply due to random events being "sifted by the blind, automatic forces of natural selection," Prof. Singer's position is certainly one logical conclusion of accepting evolution.

But then, there's more. Once having accepted that evolution is true, he then can assert that Darwinism has "stripped humanity of the special status that Judeo-Christian thought had conferred upon it," and therefore (as if that conclusion were not bad enough), "human life has *no meaning and purpose."* Prof. Singer is able to insist that *we have no purpose,* because 1) "biological life began in a *chance* [random] combination of gasses," (i.e., abiogenesis) and then 2) it "evolved through random mutation and natural selection."

Thus, followed to its logical end point, Darwin's "denial of purpose" can only lead to the conclusion that there is no God, that everything only has the "appearance of design," not actual design. And without an underlying purpose, accepting Darwin's view implies that the entire universe is just one "vast amoral machine." Worse, it reduces the unique human being that God created and gave His own breath to (Gen. 2:7), to nothing more than "a lump of matter, a collection of atoms and molecules," which is no different than any other matter in the universe.

And, as pointed out by Oswald Chambers and G.K. Chesterton, that position puts man in command of his own destiny, freeing him from the worry of having to give an account to God (Heb. 4:13) and allowing him to believe in anything he wants. What is the potential outcome of these end points? Just this: man can become his own "god."

But—*those* outcomes can happen only if God is nullified. And purposeless evolution, proclaimed as "true" and "fact," is just the vehicle to achieve them.

Thus in the final analysis, godless evolution and Creation have no common ground but are locked in a spiritual battle. What Paul teaches in 2 Cor. 6:14–15 is clear in this regard:

> "For what do righteousness and wickedness have in common? Or what fellowship can light have with darkness? What harmony is there between Christ and Belial [Satan]?" (2 Cor. 6:14–15)

**Creation's Challenges to Evolution.** Evolution *cannot* establish itself as "truth," as "fact," and be in charge as long as God stands in its way. God directly opposes all such efforts.

But, as you've probably guessed, there is a "glitch" in this push to eliminate God: *evolution cannot and will never be able to provide demonstrated evidence supporting and validating it as true* as required by the science it claims to be. The biology of life and the physiological requirement that every life process be integrated with every other one to maintain stable biological processes in a cell or organism (homeostasis) does not allow evolution to ever have occurred.

Further, given the spiritual nature of this conflict of God versus non-god, the stakes in its outcome are beyond comprehension and earthly understanding. Keep clearly in mind that if evolution is to claim that it is "fact" and "truth," then the evidence it presents must be so clear and so convincing that it is beyond dispute.

Moreover, if we take evolution at its word that it is:

- "one of the most robust and widely accepted principles of modern science,"
- an entirely secular science based on inference and circumstantial evidence with no direct experimental evidence,
- devoid of and excludes any consideration of God's Creation as shown by Intelligent Design and Irreducible Complexity,
- taught as "fact" despite unanswerable limitations inherent in its process and evidence . . .

Then, for *all of these reasons*, evolution's assertions must be challenged. And most especially, evolution appears to leave no other option than for us to make these challenges bluntly and explicitly, because of the "*signal refusal of Darwin's defenders*" to acknowledge and appropriately respond to "scientific critiques."

Therefore, evolution must answer at least five challenges based on the rigorous, objective, unbiased scientific process it claims as its foundation:

- Show us your *direct evidence* for acclaiming evolution as fact by creating a new organism with new genetic information (i.e., one with a unique genome) via experimentation as science requires, not from inference based on potentially biased human reason.

- Show us that you can create a free-living cell from a strictly random process to validate abiogenesis, a cell that has a complete DNA genome and that meets life's seven requirements. The random foundation for evolution cannot be considered remotely possible unless this feat is accomplished.

- Show us that you understand, can explain, and can replicate the specific biological *process* of an entirely new animal forming from an existing one as a result of strictly random mutations, such as the postulated case of the modern long-necked giraffe arising from a short-necked ancestor.

- Show us that you understand, can explain, and can replicate the random process of an entirely new *group* of animals forming from an existing one, such as mammals evolving from reptiles.

- Show us that evolution is a strictly rational, factual science by clearly, concisely, and in context unapologetically stating the critical limitations to the theory of evolution, along with their significance, in any presentation, textbook, or classroom— namely, that there is:

    —*no* direct evidence to support and validate abiogenesis

    —*no* direct biological evidence to support the contention that a new animal or animal group could ever arise from an existing one by a series of random events

Therefore, in all fairness and intellectual honesty, in light of these challenges and because of these limitations, evolution should state that it is nothing more than speculation, because it has *no* direct evidence to conclude anything to the contrary.

Lastly, because evolution cannot rationally and substantially claim that it is anything more than speculation (despite being supported by a "scientific consensus"), it should welcome unfettered, equal teaching and presentation of Biblical Creation to find the truth of life, teaching that at the least offers complete evidence supporting Intelligent Design and Irreducible Complexity by those most qualified to do so.

That it does not, and apparently *will* not do this, confirms its true purpose: to nullify God.

However, we need to keep at least two things clearly in mind whenever we see evolution attempting to nullify our God from our lives.

First, He is sovereign in the fullest, most complete and absolute sense of the word. Witness what He said through the prophet Nehemiah; not only did He create, but the heavenly host *bows down* before Him, as will we:

> "You alone are the LORD. You have made the heavens, The heaven of heavens with all their host, The earth and all that is on it, The seas and all that is in them. You give life to all of them, And the heavenly host bows down before You" (Neh. 9:6; NASB).

Second, no one will make the fool of God. Paul makes this axiom clear in his letter to the church in Galatia:

> "Do not be deceived: God is not mocked, for whatever one sows, that will he also reap" (Gal. 6:7; ESV).

May those who unthinkingly proclaim random evolution as truth come to know, understand, and love the One they are dedicated to declaring a nonentity. Especially for those who would hear and listen, God gently and lovingly calls to them to come to Him:

> "Come now, and let us reason together," Says the LORD, "Though your sins are as scarlet, They will be as white as snow; Though they are red like crimson, They will be like wool." (Is. 1:18, NASB)

"Come now, let us reason together . . . " A loving Father putting his arm around the shoulder of one of His children as they walk along, trying to talk some sense into them. This shows the love of Jesus and the inspiration of the Holy Spirit in drawing those separated from Him to Him.

That is what God would have of His Creation.

# CHAPTER 10

# ECCLESIASTES 12:13

*"Now all has been heard;*
*here is the conclusion of the matter:*
*Fear God and keep his commandments,*
*for this is the duty of all mankind."*

Ecclesiastes 12:13

When Solomon wrote, "Now all has been heard; here is the conclusion of the matter . . . ," he had no idea how God might be using what he wrote in the future. But Hebrews 4:12 tells us that, "the Word of God is *alive* and *powerful*" (Heb. 4:12, NLT), so we should not be surprised at how God's words apply here.

Evolution has no direct evidence to allow it to categorically assert that it is fact—none. Rather, it infers itself as such from circumstantial evidence, such as observations of fossils, similarities of DNA between obviously related organisms, and homologies across unrelated groups of animals. Further, it refuses to acknowledge any consideration that life could be created from thoroughly researched Creation efforts such as Intelligent Design and Irreducible Complexity.

Why this resistance? One obvious answer lies in its interaction with secularism, which we found earlier. But when it uses the neutral tool of science to justify its position, it doesn't take into account that many scientists do not believe that randomness is the basis for all of the natural world that we see and know. They know that there is something more, even if they can't measure it and categorize it.

Consider this quote attributed to one who might be considered the dean of all scientists, Albert Einstein. Dr. Einstein would appear to have predicted and be in full agreement with Dr. Meyer's Intelligent Design argument, when he characterized anyone who seriously pursues science as becoming convinced that the universe is made up of more than what we can see:

> "The scientists' religious feeling takes the form of a rapturous amazement at the harmony of natural law, which reveals an intelligence of such superiority that, compared with it, all the systematic thinking and acting of human beings is an utterly insignificant reflection."

Note that Einstein indirectly refers to our Creative God when he acknowledges that the natural world reveals "an intelligence of such superiority" against which human reasoning is "utterly insignificant." This musing by perhaps the greatest and most esteemed of all scientists shows that he was humbled before that which he could not explain, could not understand. Is this possible? A scientist humbling himself before God? Unquestionably so. But—understand that the face of evolution from the initial writings of Darwin through those of today's supporters would have to flatly reject Einstein's position. More than that, Einstein's position would be heresy.

For us? Would that we might all share Einstein's sense of awe at the least.

Perhaps those who reject that God could have been involved with Creation simply can't imagine One who could do such a thing. Perhaps they could be counseled with the title of the volume biblical translator J.B. Phillips wrote in 1952, *Your God Is Too Small*. If that were the stumbling block, that the God they envision is limited in some manner, are there Scriptures that they might consider? The Bible offers an abundance of comfort showing that we have a God no one can understand or conceive of except through who Jesus is and what He taught us. Consider these few verses of many. (I have collected somewhere close to 100 of them.)

The very first five words of the Bible surpass our reason and senses; they are elegant and yet full of the mystery and the love of God who is beyond our understanding:

"In the beginning God created . . ." (Gen. 1:1).

Also, the apostle Paul says (my emphasis):

"Now to him who is able to do *immeasurably* more than all we ask or *imagine* . . ." (Eph. 3:20).

*"Immeasurably more"* than we can *imagine!* Who is this God that created us? We can understand only what He reveals to us. Genesis 1:1 tells us that God was present at the beginning of all we see and know. And then, the writer of the Letter to the Hebrews proclaims that He will be there *after* all created things are gone (my emphasis):

"In the beginning, Lord, you laid the foundations of the earth, and the heavens are the work of your hands. They will perish, *but you remain* . . ." (Heb. 1:10-11a).

Recall that Darwin was set on demonstrating the purposelessness of life, a position that has so captivated individuals such as Prof. Singer of Princeton. This view is a polar opposite from who our God actually is, One who is purposeful beyond our comprehension, as Paul noted in his first letter to the Corinthian church:

"For God is not a God of disorder, but of peace" (1 Cor. 14:33a).

Ironically, those who proclaim science as the only path to being able to explain everything apparently do not understand that *Christianity made science possible.* How, if they are correct, can this be? As explained by Chuck Colson (my emphasis):

"Christianity depicted God as a 'rational, responsive, dependable, and omnipotent being' who created a universe with a

'*rational, lawful, stable*' structure. These beliefs uniquely led
to 'faith in the possibility of science.'"

For those who hold evolution to be the answer to all life, recall God's invitation from Isaiah with an open mind: "Come now,
let us reason together." God is waiting through Our Lord Jesus to
welcome *you*.

# ADVANCED SCIENCE IMPACTING EVOLUTION

Appendix I deals in greater depth with four science or non-science issues that can impact the manner in which evolution might be taught, presented, promoted, or challenged. Although perhaps interesting in and of itself, all of the material in this section has but one purpose and goal: to be applied to and illustrate the deficiencies inherent in the "science" evolution proclaims as true, in the "facts" it offers as gospel.

These topics involve:

- Skepticism: The Hallmark of Good Science
- Experimental Design: Theories and Hypotheses in Practice
- Post-normal Science
- Scientism

## SKEPTICISM: THE HALLMARK OF GOOD SCIENCE

Skepticism is a critical aspect of science for two reasons, the first of which is that it helps a scientist (or anyone else, for that matter) grow in how they think about observations they make of the natural world. Because no one experiment, no set of experiments, no set of observations is complete in and of itself—ever—science requires careful and critical thinking to try to find flaws, errors, or incomplete information in any assertion, claims, or conclusions. Skepticism in science, then, first of all implies the need for the discipline of critical thinking.

Secondly, and perhaps more importantly, there is the matter of completeness of data or observations. One foundational character-istic of *any* set of data obtained from any type of science study, *any* conclusion drawn from such a study, or *any* theory developed from observations or experiments is that the matter investigated is *never* settled, *never* final, no matter how many experiments have been suc-cessful or how much data has been gathered.

**Scientists Must Be Skeptics About Their Work.** A good scientist must *always* be open to new information, that is, be a skeptic. In that regard, the scientist must always have some level of doubt about the certainty and completeness of his or her work to at least some degree, because no one can ever know everything about anything. Thus, a scientist should not automatically take for granted that something someone asserts or claims is "right." Rather, scientists may always ques-tion or withhold their approval until such time as they are *reasonably* convinced of the truth of a proposition. All of the following examples point to and reinforce this need for caution.

Dr. Richard Feynman cautions anyone who becomes involved in science as to why skepticism is paramount:

> "The first principle [of science] is that you must *not* fool your-self—and you are the easiest person to fool."

Dr. Feynman expanded the reason for being cautious at another time—the need to leave room for doubt (my emphasis):

> "Authority may be a *hint* as to what the truth is but is not the *source* of information . . . We must *absolutely* leave room for doubt, or there is no progress and no learning. There is no learning without having to pose a question. And a question requires doubt."

Consider too again this cautionary quote from 19th century English biologist Thomas Huxley (1825–1895), the one known as "Darwin's Bulldog" (my emphasis):

"The evidence . . . however properly reached, may always be more or less wrong, the best information being *never* complete, and the best reasoning being liable to fallacy."

Finally, recall Einstein's reason for being skeptical:

"No amount of experimentation can ever prove me right; a single experiment can prove me wrong."

Note how the two parts of Einstein's insight reinforce each other and how he uses the word "prove" in each (my emphasis): "*No* amount of experimentation can ever *prove* me right . . . " "A *single* experiment can *prove* me wrong."

Take a moment to more deeply reflect on Einstein's statement. Einstein's comment is an absolute and true statement that uncovers a key limitation of any natural science: you can never *prove* anything in the natural world to be "right" through experimentation or observation, even though that's the way science is performed. Further information can show, without question, that you are wrong.

Note, too, that science does not and cannot "prove" something in the sense of a proof offered in mathematics. Rather, any "proof" is only the best and most complete answer that can be given based on the data available at the time the answer was made.

Rather, it has also been pointed out that, "*Unlike history,* [any] physical science [such as biology], is a discipline that is validated differently—through *future* observation." This one feature—*the ability to predict*—has particular application to evolution theory and must be applied any time evolutionary theory is attempted to be validated.

The bottom line of this limitation inherent in any natural science is that the matter is *never* settled. Full, complete knowledge of any part of the natural world can *never* be known by anyone. Therefore, a scientist must be skeptical about making absolute conclusions. A scientist must assume there is always potentially something *more* to be discovered and at least be open to being shown that he or she is wrong. Thus, any scientist must always remain alert to allow for that *one* experiment, that *one* unknown piece of the puzzle that shows them to be—there is no other appropriate word—wrong. This insight should weigh on any scientist and humble them. It makes it clear that a scientist is *never* the final authority of anything.

This last point was solidly brought home to me some years back by my grandson, who was eight years old at the time, as he and I were walking along the beach one day. He asked me a question regarding something we saw, and I had to admit that I didn't know. "But, Poppie," he said, "you're a scientist! Scientists know *everything*!" No, we don't; no one does, regardless of their education, training, or profession . . .

**Implications of Skepticism.** Along with Dr. Feynman, both Huxley's and Einstein's cautions lead to this first important implication, if not another critical absolute: science *cannot* be dogmatic in any statements of fact regarding the natural world. It must leave the door open to new findings and reinterpretation of past data. Therefore, the work of science should *never* state nor promote *any* conclusions in dogmatic terms that exclude the possibility the work might be wrong. For any scientist to assert that something is proved or that the matter is settled implies an absolute determination, and therefore, such an attitude in itself is just plain wrong. No matter how well accepted, all scientific theory is subject to change at the next experiment or when the next bit of information comes to light.

**Being Absolute Leads to Demagoguery.** What is demagoguery at its core and what is the problem with it? Sometimes clarity comes from the most interesting sources and can be directly applied to science. For example, online Hot Air commentator Ed Morrissey has noted that (my emphasis):

> "Demagoguery doesn't work because of *rational* arguments and evidence. It usually works in contravention to both, since one doesn't need demagoguery when the facts are on one's side. Demagoguery works in ignorance of facts and rationality by playing on fear and emotion."

Recall that those who propose *any* theory in science are completely responsible for defending it to those who are skeptical. If it is not possible to offer data obtained through experimentation or observation that confirms the theory and repudiates the criticism, then the one who proposes the theory must either withhold the theory, modify it, discard it, withdraw it, or admit that it is *only* speculation until such time as the needed information is obtained. It is *not* incumbent on those critical of the theory to propose an alternative theory or explanation, although they can certainly can and frequently do so to the benefit of the body of science work. But, the onus to defend is always with those who propose or support.

**A Final Note.** We leave our discussion of skepticism in science with an interesting statement Carl Sagan made in a 1990 interview:

> "Science is more than a body of knowledge. It is a way of thinking; a way of skeptically interrogating the universe with a fine understanding of human fallibility."

Yes, science certainly involves a way of analyzing and reasoning that is (or should be) disciplined and demanding (evangelist Oswald Chambers defined it as "systematized common sense"). But the key to actually *working* in science is in itself much more. Science depends on rigorously applying a well-defined and specific methodology to obtain as true results as possible. No natural science, such as evolution claims to be, is exempt.

## EXPERIMENTAL DESIGN: THEORIES AND HYPOTHESES IN PRACTICE

Evolution claims to be a proven theory. So, following the axiom Dr. Feynman laid down—that your "guess" requires experiment to find out if you're right—how does validating a theory by experiment work in practice, and how is it tested with specific hypotheses? This section introduces you to selected examples that illustrate some basic principles of experimental design. These will clearly shed light on the seemingly insurmountable experimental hurdles that evolution faces in being validated with direct, definitive evidence.

Up first, the basic "A" versus "B" test, a basic type of experimental design. We will apply the basic principles of this experimental design to more sophisticated studies, and then we will look at a critical observational study type of experiment in physics.

**The "A" versus "B" test.** At one time, my wife and I had three identical outdoor chairs on our back porch. Each had a white metal frame with yellow synthetic fabric for the seat and back. Unfortunately, unsightly gray mold had a tendency to grow on them during the summer in the humid environment in which we live. A little bleach solution, some brushing, and letting them sit in the sun to dry cured the problem—temporarily. After a few weeks, either my wife or I had to repeat the process.

Enter a commercial spray product advertized as a "Mold and Mildew Inhibitor." How does that tie in to forming a theory and then developing hypotheses? It does so by giving us a graphic example of how a test by design experiment works.

We will start at the most basic level and progress to an overview illustrating more carefully controlled laboratory-oriented type experimental designs. The purpose? To gain a basic foundation, a set of standards to understand the extreme problems faced by evolutionary biologists if they were to attempt to test abiogenesis and evolution. It will also serve to highlight the attention to detail needed in day-to-day science.

**Basic Experiments.** Our first experiment follows a preliminary test that to very simply determine whether the spray might work or not. We cleaned the chairs, sprayed them with the inhibitor, and let them sit in the sun to dry. Over the succeeding weeks, they seemed to stay clean longer than they did before they were sprayed. Practically speaking, that was all the information we needed to continue to use the product. We had good reason to infer that it worked. (Yes, we were able to confidently infer a conclusion.)

But how could that result be validated to gain direct evidence in a science experiment? Preliminary results showed it likely to work, and so that is our hypothesis and our prediction, consistent with the standards of the scientific method. In the "A versus B" test, we add a control group. To do this, we spray (treat) two of the chairs with the mold inhibitor, let them dry, and then let them sit outside as usual in the same environment. The third chair remains untreated and serves as a control. Let us assume that the mold returns to the control chair first, while the treated chairs remain mold-free for a longer duration of time. In terms of science, what have we done?

In point of fact, what we actually did was to test the initial stage of a theory, the theory being that a compound (or compounds) in the spray inhibits the mold, and will do so wherever it is used. Because we previously had *no* evidence that the theory is true, we had to gather data by experiment (i.e., direct evidence) to either support it or to show it to be false. In practice, we did so by starting with two hypotheses.

- Hypothesis 1: This hypothesis predicts that the product does *not* work. More formally, this hypothesis is known as the "Null" or "no effect" hypothesis. Although it derives from statistics, it is useful here to help understand accepting or rejecting a hypothesis and theory on the basis of experimental data. Our critical criterion for the Null hypothesis in this example is that the mold would return in about the same amount of time that it did without the spray treatment, i.e., the product didn't work.

- Hypothesis 2: This hypothesis predicts that the product *does* work. Formally, this hypothesis is known as the alternative hypothesis. Our criterion here is that mold will *not* return as quickly.

The scientific method requires that one of these two hypotheses be rejected on the basis of the data obtained (whereas the other would be accepted). In our example, our mold product appeared to work; the mold did not return on the sprayed ("treated") chairs as quickly as we expected. Therefore, we reject the Null hypothesis for this experiment;

in formal terms, it was "falsified." That leaves us with the alternate hypothesis (i.e., "it worked!"), which we accept as true and move on.

The "it worked hypothesis" needs to be tested further before we can feel comfortable that what we found is real. Why? First of all, by doing more testing, we're *confirming* our first findings, an important part of the scientific method. To get "picky," we have a number of options, and if we were the spray manufacturer, we might use them. Here are a few to illustrate how we might go about this:

- **Use more chairs.** To gain an acceptable statistical analysis, we need to increase the number of chairs per group to anywhere between six (if the response is uniform) and ten or more (if the response were relatively variable). This step is likely sufficient for the type of product we are testing, but if not . . .

- **Randomize the chairs.** We can assume, but have no guarantee, that the chairs were constructed or would act uniformly to the spray due to a variety of factors. Therefore, chairs should be randomly assigned to control and treated groups. This step helps ensure that any variability in the manufacture of the chairs would be equally spread between our control and treated groups and would give us confidence to trust that any activity we might see is real. Lastly, we could . . .

- **Read the results "blind."** Recall that every scientist is biased to some degree about any experiment they might perform or theory they might hold as true. How can that fact be minimized or even overcome? In reading the results of a "blind" experiment, those who visually determine the presence of mold in the control and treated chairs would have no idea which chairs belonged to which groups; they would not be part of setting up the experiment. Further, each chair could be coded and then randomized following treatment, forcing the observer to read the results in an unbiased manner as possible.

Gaining a true result in this manner to formally reject one hypothesis and accept the other is the general principle that drives designed experimentation in science, and it is a solid means of providing direct evidence. Can it be sophisticated? Absolutely, as the two study designs used in clinical trials will show.

**Advanced experimental designs.** The specific experimental methods that theoretical and applied science employ obviously must fit the needs of any particular project. They can be relatively simple or quite complex but are always *rigorous* to ensure—as much as possible—that the results:

1. *exclude* any variable that might "muddy" the results, and

2. *accurately* reflect the truth of the piece of the natural world investigated

The dedication of scientists in unsnarling difficult questions to find answers is sometimes quite stunning. The three *very brief* examples below were selected to give you a "feel" for what could be involved in scientific investigations. The takeaway of these examples is not the example itself, although each is interesting. Rather, I am including these to help you appreciate the deficiencies and lack of critical documentary evidence used to support evolution.

Keep in mind that the chair examples, as well as each of the two clinical studies below, show the following *principles* of the scientific method. These principles are critical to our critique of evolution, which is *not* exempt from them:

1. Their designs are *purposeful.*

2. The designs will predict and *demonstrate* a *specific* outcome.

3. The outcome is *unknown* before the study is performed.

4. The data obtained will provide direct evidence of an effect (or lack of effect).

5. Direct evidence does *not* need *inference* to reach a conclusion.

We will first look at clinical studies that illustrate applied science investigation, an advanced Phase 3 study for a new drug and then a specialized "double-blind, double-dummy" clinical study. Both expand the principles you found earlier in the "yellow chair" experiment. Again, keep in mind that the principles and standards employed in these studies apply equally to how the biological processes of evolution should be tested. Examples of designed observational studies will illustrate the careful and dedicated effort that can sometimes be required in science to validate a theory. These document the search for and the finding of the cystic fibrosis gene, and the incredible effort used to find elementary physics particle, the Higgs boson.

**Clinical studies.** In the yellow chair examples, we saw the "control versus treated" type design common to many biological studies. Clinical studies, especially advanced (e.g., Phase 3 for drug approval) clinical studies, well illustrate these principles, but in a more sophisticated manner. Keep in mind that regardless of the level of complexity and sophistication, all fields of science require rigorous standards in any investigation.

In a Phase 3 clinical study, a large patient population (e.g., 500 to 1,000 plus patients) is recruited according to pre-planned design criteria. These criteria are very specific as to the disease characteristics of those who can and those who cannot be included, so that *every* non-essential variable is excluded in so far as possible. No changes are made to the criteria once they are approved. Patients who participate are *randomly* selected from that patient population, and then *randomly* assigned to receive the drug, a particular dose of the drug, or not receive it at all (placebo controls).

Enter the "double-blind" design. This design is a common feature of many such clinical studies. In this case, *neither* the clinical staff *nor* the patients participating know who has been assigned to receive the active drug or treatment. Patients who do not receive the active drug receive a placebo, a "treatment" which in every respect (e.g., size, color, taste, etc) is *identical* to the active treatment. The entire purpose of this approach is to minimize bias in both patient reporting of drug effects (therapeutic effects and side effects) and the clinical staff in monitoring and assessing those effects. Bottom line: the double-blind design is a rigorous attempt to gain the most accurate results; it keeps everyone honest by "blinding" them to what's going on.

But what do you do when you want to compare effectiveness of two drugs that might have different dose schedules (e.g., daily versus weekly), colors, sizes, shapes (e.g., blue versus white capsules/tablets, small versus large, oblong versus round), etc.? Enter the "double-dummy" (i.e., parallel design) feature of a double-blind trial. In this case, every patient receives *two* (or more) treatments, one active and the other a placebo, where every placebo is identical to the active treatment in how it is dosed, size, shape, color, etc.

How do these clinical study examples relate to evolution gaining direct evidence to help validate it? To even attempt to demonstrate that it is the science and fact as it asserts, evolution has a very rigorous and obstacle-strewn path to follow. At the least, it would have to adhere to accepted standards of experimental design in any work it presented to validate the process required to show that either abiogenesis or emergence of new animals from existing ones in any designed experiment it uses.

**Observational studies.** Given the complexity of the biological processes required for abiogenesis and evolution to ever have occurred randomly, an "A versus B" type study might not be universally applicable for its purposes. Observational studies by design that predict a specific result might be more appropriate. I have included examples of two such studies next. Each of these provided direct evidence in their outcome validating a specific theory. Evolution would do well to consider developing such studies for its purposes.

**A Research Study to Find the Gene for Cystic Fibrosis.** Cystic fibrosis is a devastating genetic disease that affects the lungs, pancreas, liver, kidneys, and intestines of those afflicted. After being involved in the human genome project, Director of the National Institutes of Health, Dr. Francis Collins, recruited teams at several research institutions to find the gene for cystic fibrosis and its location that was theorized on a specific chromosome. It took these individuals *two and* *one-half years* working collaboratively, and multiple, multiple experiments (and failures) to eventually find and *document* it. Keep this level of dedication in mind when considering evolution, because, apart from those in prebiotic chemistry, it has *no* such experiments to offer as evidence.

**Identifying the Higgs boson particle.** Over forty years ago, a physics theory *predicted* finding a specific and very elusive sub-atomic particle of matter, the Higgs boson, or the "God particle." Billions of dollars went into this research to engineer, build, and operate a particle accelerator seventeen miles in circumference in Switzerland to find and demonstrate it. The Higgs boson was finally found, confirmed as to its predicted physical characteristics, and reported in July, 2012.

How great was the effort to discover the Higgs boson? Over 10,000 scientists and engineers from 100 countries collaborated in this effort, along with hundreds of research institutions and universities.

If evidence of the Higgs boson had never been obtained, the theory hypothesizing its existence could never be stated as having been validated (i.e., as being *fact*), at least until the time that it was found. It would remain an intriguing possibility, a supposition, but *not* a fact.

Can evolution claim attempts at such dedicated and rigorous testing that in any way would validate its two claims for abiogenesis and evolution of new animals? Specifically, that a free-living cell such as the LUCA ever developed randomly by creating one? And beyond that demonstration, can it demonstrate random mutations as the basis for the proposed progressive transformation of that first cell to the diversity of life we see, especially humans? It has not done so yet.

## POST-NORMAL SCIENCE

Post-normal science can be used as a cultural wedge, because it mixes science and politics. As you have gathered by now, the core scientific method is designed and set up as a *neutral* tool to determine what is demonstrably true (i.e., what is real) in the natural world and what is not. The examples of clinical trials we discussed previously show the care and rigor necessary to test whether a new drug is safe and effective, characterizing all of its effects as closely as possible to maximize benefit to a patient.

But, whether we are dealing with a clinical trial, a laboratory experiment, or an observational field study, this process takes the form of stating a theory and then a hypothesis, and then developing data *by experiment or observation* to show if what you're thinking—your hypothesis—is correct, that it is true (and if so, to what degree). Or it will show if it is essentially wrong, in which case, it is falsified. When sufficient confirmed and validated data are obtained, a theory may be developed to explain some phenomenon, if appropriate. In as far as possible as you know, this process must be *independent* of any bias or outside influence of the investigator or others involved. Post-normal science moves away from this objective process into the realm of subjectivity.

Post-normal science appears to derive from philosophical discussions dealing with situations where, "facts are uncertain, values in dispute, stakes high, and decisions urgent," such as might be faced during a difficult surgical procedure. Further, it is developed to deal with "issue driven science relating to the protection of health and the environment," and to bring in an "extended peer community" and "extended facts," thus further removing itself from core scientific method principles into ideologies masquerading as science. In other words, science is subordinated to policy implementation or ideology.

President Dwight D. Eisenhower foresaw the damaging potential for post-normal science some 55 years ago when he said (my emphasis),

> "Yet in holding scientific discovery in respect, as we should, we must also be alert to the equal and opposite danger that *public policy could itself become the captive of a scientific-technological elite.*"

We are beginning to witness this outcome today.

**Post-normal science and public policy.** Although the description of post-normal science is somewhat vague (a clue that it is *not* science), it appears to be being used for applying scientific knowledge to *public policy*. Knowledge in this instance is not a demonstrated "yes" or "no" obtained by experiment, but is considered "provisional" and subject to change " . . . through its *interaction with society.*"

**Post-normal science and evolution.** Post-normal science is likely to have an impact on how evolution is presented and accepted. Witness this quote from a recent editorial in the journal *Science* by the CEO of the AAAS (excerpted; my emphasis):

> "There is no shortage of topics where *policy-makers* or other *members of the public* seem to persistently misunderstand, misrepresent, or disregard the underlying science: . . . evolution, among others."

The writer of the article concerning the editorial makes a very credible speculation that the intent appears to be for "scientists [to] *turn from facts to ideology,* cultural identity, and framing to move public opinion. . ."

Again, this is not science as it should be applied to determining whether evolution is true or not. Given the position of the AAAS presented previously, it is no surprise that attempts are being made to move evolution into post-normal science. It cannot do that and remake our culture, our moral standards and ideals without nullifying God first.

## SCIENTISM—SCIENCE MIMING THE AUTHORITY OF A RELIGION

Sometimes when I read articles about evolution, I get the feeling that a particular biological science, like the claimed formation of the universe devoid of God's Creation, is viewed as some sort of mysterious, majestic, beneficent universal cosmic force, as Carl Sagan implied when he said, "The Cosmos is all that is, or was, or ever will be," as you found earlier. That we should stand in awe of it, have obeisance to it, bow down, and worship it. Or, at the least, stand in awe of the science and scientists who explain it. It is as though man, and *not* God, becomes the measure and judge of all things, completely in line with secularism.

In popular media and periodicals, scientists have routinely been given an almost mystical accord. Article after article is published in our popular news media noting that "Scientists say that . . . " Such types of statements passively give "science" an unchallenged aura of authority that "they" know what they are talking about, and the rest of us should just listen, take note, and act accordingly.

But, do these statements really reflect science? Recall the rigorous standards of how science is done. So, such statements imply that careful research has been done, all facts gathered, checked, analyzed, and critiqued, and unbiased conclusions made. However, even if that were to be the case, *so what*? Rather, as we know by now, *no* answer given by science is absolute. New or additional data may change conclusions or show them to be inaccurate; methodology may have not been adequate, etc., etc.

The bottom line is that science does *not* have and should *never* be accorded quasi-religious authority, and further, it should *never* be treated as if it did. No one should bow down and worship at the altar of science. That said, evolution (which author Phillip Johnson has identified as "Darwinist Religion)" appears to be being promoted as the first exception.

Such an approach clearly falls under the mantle of scientism, which has been characterized as follows by author Austin L. Hughes, Carolina Distinguished Professor of Biological Sciences at the University of South Carolina:

> "Advocates of scientism today claim the sole mantle of rationality, frequently equating science with reason itself. Yet it seems the very antithesis of reason to insist that . . . science and science alone can answer longstanding questions . . . gives rise to countless problems."

Phillip Johnson and Austin Hughes are not alone in emphasizing scientism's disturbing viewpoints. In a CNS News article, Eric Metaxas points out, "Writing in the *London Times*, Melanie Phillips suggests we've entered a kind of scientific 'dark age,'" referring to the firestorm resulting from the *PLoS One* article over the design of the hand showing the work of the Creator that you read earlier. She then is reported as noting, "Underlying much of this disarray . . . is surely the pressure to conform to an idea, whether political, commercial or ideological." The article continues, "From the Christian view, that idea is called 'scientism,' the notion that science *alone* offers truth about our world." It then emphasizes Phillips' conclusion:

> "Scientists [today] pose as secular priests. . . . They alone, they claim, hold the keys to the universe."

Never lose sight of what science is: It is an excellent tool developed from human reason and experience, an elegant, sophisticated tool to find out what is true about the natural world. It cannot explain Creation nor give us moral values. It cannot save us. All it can do is to describe the physical universe we see.

# SCIENCE PROBLEMS THAT IMPACT ABIOGENESIS

Prebiotic chemistry experiments take place in a clean laboratory environment where everything involving those experiments is controlled. In nature, that is never the case. In this brief section, we will be looking at two physical laws that would directly affect any reactions needed for abiogenesis to occur as well as speculating on how the random environment could actually *stop* any life from forming.

## LAW OF MASS ACTION

Like other physical laws, the Law of Mass Action can be somewhat overwhelming if it is considered in detail. For our purposes, one part of it directly affects abiogenesis—the concentration of various chemicals needed for the reaction to occur at all. These are commonly known as the reactants.

The Law of Mass Action states that "the rate of a chemical reaction is directly proportional to the molecular concentrations of the reacting substances." In other words, if all reactants were in perfect concentrations, and all other factors (e.g., temperature, acid/base balance, pressure) were optimal, a chemical reaction would occur at its maximum rate. But if one (or more) reactants were at a suboptimal concentration, the reaction would go slowly or might not occur at all.

In a laboratory, all conditions for a chemical reaction can be controlled. That is not the case in the random natural environment in which abiogenesis would have to have occurred. It is virtually certain that reactants needed to produce amino acids and other biochemicals needed for the first cell would not have been in useful, let alone optimal, concentrations at any time. This situation is further impacted by other physical laws, particularly Fick's Laws of Diffusion.

## FICK'S LAWS OF DIFFUSION

A lightning bolt strikes a pond or other water (aqueous) environment. Let's assume for a moment that, according to prebiotic chemistry experiments such as those performed by Miller-Urey, some amino acids and perhaps nucleic acid biochemical precursors are formed. Let's assume further that the water will not dry up, otherwise, no life could form.

Fick's Laws of Diffusion mandate that whatever amount of prebiotic chemicals were produced will diffuse away from the point of their formation. Specifically, the molecules will diffuse from the area of high concentration where they were formed into areas of lower concentration or where there are none.

In other words, any prebiotically formed chemicals would continue to be diluted until the entire body of water contains the same concentration of them. Imagine the virtually insignificant amount that would be found in a small pond—or a body of water the size of a Great Lake, or an ocean. And, if the water was in motion (e.g., a creek, a river, an ocean), that process would occur rapidly.

Now, combine this limitation with those associated with the Law of Mass Action. Specifically, consider that if there is an insufficient amount of one (or more) compounds needed for a chemical reaction to take place according to the Law of Mass Action, the reaction simply doesn't happen, or happens so slowly that it yields no product.

Combined, the Law of Mass Action and Fick's Laws of Diffusion virtually preclude abiogenesis from ever occurring. Are there any other possible limiting physical factors that would affect the random formation of life? Yes, and we will look at one more next.

## ANTIMETABOLITES

As you found earlier, abiogenesis, like evolution, depends entirely on an unspecified and untold number of random events yielding the first free-living cell. Prebiotic chemistry experiments have successfully yielded amino acids, short random protein chains, and some nucleic acid bases, all of which are speculated to have somehow come together and yielded life. All well and good as a speculation, but the requirement that all events are *random* raises an interesting problem: What if some of the compounds formed by that random process—especially the nucleic acid bases—were sufficiently different that they were *toxic* to the process of life, especially RNA and DNA synthesis? No such compounds have been reported from prebiotic experiments, but results from those studies do *not* apparently include any search for them. So, if any were formed, they would not have been found.

The key question to ask is this: Are such compounds known? Because if some have been identified today for experimental or medical uses, then—given the disconnected random events involved in abiogenesis—Darwin's primordial soup could well have contained unknown ones. That distinct possibility cannot be discounted, because compounds that inhibit DNA synthesis and other cell functions at multiple levels are in fact well known: the antimetabolite class of anticancer drugs.

Antimetabolites constitute a therapeutic group of over twenty different anticancer drugs. Any drug in this class interferes with the metabolism of a cell in a manner that inhibits DNA replication or other cellular functions leading to its death. It can do so because it mimics a normal cell metabolite, but it cannot be used by the cell. So, an antimetabolite in essence is used by the cell, but it "gums up the works." As a result the cell is inhibited and can either no longer divide, or it simply dies. Because cancer cells multiply more rapidly than most normal cells, these drugs are reasonably specific in attacking cancer and have use treating a wide variety of tumors. We will look at two such agents: 5-fluorouracil (floor-oh-YOO- rah-sil) and cytarabine (sigh-TAHR-uh-been).

**5-Fluorouracil.** 5-fluorouracil (5-FU) is one of the better known antimetabolite drugs. It is similar to the RNA nucleic acid base uracil, but with a fluorine molecule attached. However, the cell uses it very differently from uracil. Its effect is primarily against DNA synthesis, but it also has secondary effects against RNA synthesis. Once incorporated in the DNA synthesis pathway, that pathway is blocked, and the cell commits suicide (apoptosis).

**Cytarabine.** Another antimetabolite agent, which is not as familiar as 5-FU, is cytarabine. To understand cytarabine, we need to talk about nucleic acid structure for a moment. Nucleic acid bases are built into RNA (ribonucleic acid) in part by being linked to a specific type of sugar, the five-carbon sugar ribose (a pentose). In the case of DNA (deoxyribonucleic acid), cell processes remove one oxygen molecule from ribose to yield deoxyribose, which is found only in living cells. Twelve natural pentose sugars are known, one of them being arabinose. Cytarabine is interesting in that it combines cytosine (a normal nucleic acid base) with arabinose to produce an extremely effective agent against certain leukemias.

What this compound (and 5-FU) illustrates so clearly is the virtually unlimited random synthetic possibilities that could have existed in Darwin's primordial soup that would have stopped abiogenesis so readily. No one can assume that that environment would have constituted the clean, controlled environment of a prebiotic chemistry experiment.

Again, abiogenesis cannot be taken for other than speculation without science producing *life*—a whole, free-living cell that meets the seven requirements for life that you found earlier. Without this direct evidence, the entirety of evolution can only be regarded as speculation, not fact.

# GLOSSARY

**Alleles (ah LEELZ):** Different physical forms of genes.

**Blood pressure (BP):** The pressure that circulating blood exerts on the walls of blood vessels. BP in arteries, which carry blood away from the heart, is higher than that in veins, which return blood to the heart.

**Coevolution:** The term coevolution is typically used to refer to two ecologically close organisms that genetically evolve "together" (i.e., "coevolve") in a mutually beneficial relationship. As applied to the giraffe, evolution considers that this animal could not have evolved its long neck without simultaneously 1) coevolving high blood pressure to push its blood up to the brain and 2) coevolving its entire cardiovascular system and organs fed by it to withstand that otherwise lethally high blood pressure.

**Direct evidence:** "Evidence that is gained by *direct demonstration,*" so that 1) it is "real, tangible, or clear" and as such, 2) it does *not* require reasoning or **inference** to draw a conclusion.

**Empirical (ehm PEER uh kuhl):** Knowledge gained by observation *and experimentation.*

**Genome (JEE nohm):** "An organism's complete set of DNA, including all of its genes. Each genome contains all of the information needed to build and maintain that organism."

**Genes:** Those parts of DNA that carry out its "instructions" to make proteins. Different physical forms of genes are called "alleles."

**Hematopoiesis (HEE mah toh poy ee sis):** The physiological process by which new blood cells are produced. Also spelled "haematopoiesis."

**Homeostasis (hoh mee oh STAY sis):** Homeostasis refers to the dynamic but stable internal environment of an organism (or single cell), and the integrated feedback and control processes by which that environment is maintained. The organism will not and cannot survive if that environment is not maintained.

**Inference:** The making of a best explanation; the drawing, or deriving a conclusion from factual information or information *assumed* to be true in the *absence* of evidence gained by *direct demonstration*; an educated guess.

**Mutation (myoo TAY shun):** Mutations permanently change (alter) the active parts of DNA, their genes. In the case of evolution, all mutations would have to be hereditary, that is, be capable of being passed on and having an effect on subsequent generations. Additionally, for mutations to make any meaningful changes and cause new animals to come to be (e.g., reptiles to mammals), the question is this: How many mutations would be required and in what order?

**Parasitology (pah rah sit AH loh gee):** The study of animal and human parasites, such as trichinosis and malaria.

**Physiology (fi zee AH loh gee):** 1) Essentially, physiology describes the study of *how* the various integrated life processes of an organism work, either at the level of the single cell (cell physiology), specific organ systems (e.g., cardiac, respiratory physiology), or globally for the whole organism (e.g., reptilian physiology; mammalian physiology). 2) The subdiscipline of biology that studies life processes of any organism in terms of its systems.

**Sequellae (see KWEL ee):** "A pathological condition resulting from a prior disease, injury, or attack." In other words, the abnormal consequences of a disease or condition.

# REFERENCES

*Note to reader: All references listed herein are in the order in which they appear in each chapter.*

## CHAPTER 1

1. Saylo, Monalie C., Cheryl C. Escoton, and Micah M. Saylo. "Punctuated equilibrium vs. phyletic gradualism." *International Journal of Bio-Science and Bio-Technology.* December 2011. Accessed March 29, 2017. http://www.sersc.org/journals/IJBSBT/vol3_no4/3.pdf.

2. Favaloro, B., et al. "Role of apoptosis in disease." *Aging.* May 31, 2012. Accessed March 29, 2017. http://www.aging-us.com/article/100459/text.

3. Strobel, Lee. 2004. "The evidence of biological information: the challenge of DNA and the origin of life." In: *The Case for a Creator.* Grand Rapids, MI: Zondervan®; 298.

4. "Evasion of apoptosis: a hallmark of cancer." Genentech: Biooncology. Accessed March 29, 2017. https://www.biooncology.com/pathways/bcl-2/evading-apoptosis.html.

## CHAPTER 2

1. Franklin, Cory. "The silencing of global warming critics." *Chicago Tribune.* May 21, 2014. Accessed March 29, 2017. http://articles.chicagotribune.com/2014-05-21/opinion/

ct-perspec-climate-0521-20140521_1_climate-scientists-climate-change-climate-debate.

2.  Ashton, John F. 2013. "Why a living cell cannot arise by chance." In: *Evolution Impossible.* Green Forest, AR: Master Books, 37.

3.  Nye, Bill. 2015. "Me You and Evolution, Too." In: *Undeniable,* ed. Corey S. Powell. New York, NY: St. Martin's Griffen, 3–5, 8.

4.  McElwee, Sean and Phillip Cohen. "The GOP vs. the pursuit of knowledge: inside the Republican crusade against science." *Salon.* April 11, 2016. Accessed March 29, 2017. http://www.salon.com/2016/04/11/the_gop_vs_the_pursuit_of_knowledge_inside_the_republican_crusade_against_science/.

5.  Gosselin, Pierre. "MEP Roger Helmer: 'Vahrenholt A star of the climate sceptic movement . . . time to reject climate alarmism.'" *No Tricks Zone.* September 15, 2012. Accessed March 29, 2017.

6.  http://notrickszone.com/2012/09/15/mep-roger-helmer-vahrenholt-a-star-of-the-climate-sceptic-movement-time-to-reject-climate-alarmism/#sthash.pj8D1nuP.dpuf.

7.  Dawkins, Karen E. "Dawkins becomes a creationist." *Creation Moments.* [undated]. Accessed March 29, 2017. http://www.creation-moments.com/node/5954.

8.  "Discovery Clarifies Soda-pop Science . . . " (Headline from Wednesday September 4, 2013 *The News and Observer,* 5B).

9.  "'Science of Beer' goes on tap . . . " (Headline from Thursday September 5, 2013 *The News and Observer,* 3B).

10. BrainyQuote: Albert Einstein. "No amount of experimentation . . . " [undated]. Accessed December 14, 2016. https://www.brainyquote.com/quotes/quotes/a/alberteins100017.html.

11. Gosselin, Pierre. "Leading expert slams consensus as 'anti-science. . . .' When You Have Consensus, You Got Trouble!" *No Tricks Zone.* February 21, 2016. Accessed December 4, 2017. http://notrickszone. com/2016/02/21/leading-expert-slams-consensus-as-anti-science-when-you-have-consensus-you-got-trouble/#sthash.8DWRp-m9T.9SpoUTJo.dpuf.

12. "Science and the Church." *New Advent Catholic Encyclopedia.* [undated]. Accessed December 5, 2016. http://www.newadvent.org/cathen/13598b.htm.

13. Popova, Maria. "Richard Feynman reveals key to science in 63 seconds." *BrainPickings.* [undated]. Accessed December 15, 2016. https://www.brainpickings.org/2012/05/11/richard-feynman-key-to-science/.

14. Heller, Tony. "Barack Obama's war on science, rational thought and freedom." *The Deplorable Climate Science Blog.* January 16, 2016. Accessed December 5, 2016. http://realclimatescience.com/2016/01/barack-obamas-war-on-science-rational-thought-and-freedom/.

15. Watts, Anthony. "A view of science worth reflecting upon." *Watts Up With That?* November 16, 2013. Accessed March 29, 2016. https://wattsupwiththat.com/2013/11/16/a-view-of-science-worth-reflecting-upon/.

16. Watts, Anthony. "Consensus climate science: What would Thomas Huxley say?" *Watts Up With That?* April 16, 2009. Accessed December 5, 2016. https://wattsupwiththat.com/2009/04/16/consensus-climate-science-what-would-thomas-huxley-say/.

17. Monckton, Christopher. "The illogic of climate hysteria." *Watts Up With That?* April 20, 2012. Accessed December 5, 2016. https://wattsupwiththat.com/2012/04/20/the-illogic-of-climate-hysteria/.

18. The Original Skeptical Raptor. "Developing and supporting a scientific consensus." *Skeptical Raptor.* May 31, 2015. Accessed March

29, 2017. http://www.skepticalraptor.com/skepticalraptorblog.php/developing-supporting-scientific-consensus/.

19. Barton, Nicholas H., et al. 2007. "Evidence for evolution." In: *Evolution.* Cold Springs Harbor, NY: Cold Spring Harbor Laboratory Press, 65.

20. Gosselin Pierre. "Leading expert slams consensus as 'anti-science. . . .' When you have consensus, you got trouble!" *No Tricks Zone.* February 21, 2016. Accessed December 4, 2017. http://notrickszone.com/2016/02/21/leading-expert-slams-consensus-as-anti-science-when-you-have-consensus-you-got-trouble/#sthash.8DWRp-m9T.9SpoUTJo.dpuf.

21. Heller, Tony. "Barack Obama's war on science, rational thought and freedom." *The Deplorable Climate Science Blog.* January 16, 2016. Accessed December 5, 2016. http://realclimatescience.com/2016/01/barack-obamas-war-on-science-rational-thought-and-freedom/.

22. Goodreads: Leo Tolstoy quotes. "Wrong does not cease to be wrong . . ." [undated]. Accessed January 2, 2017. http://www.goodreads.com/quotes/106513-wrong-does-not-cease-to-be-wrong-because-the-majority.

23. "Using some common terms carefully and accurately in scientific speech and writing." [undated]. Accessed December 5, 2016. http://oregonstate.edu/instruction/bb317/scientifictheories.html.

24. American Association for the Advancement of Science. [Untitled letter to OK Sen. Straton Taylor] March 20, 2006. Accessed December 5, 2016. http://www.aaas.org/sites/default/files/migrate/uploads/0322ok.pdf.

25. Goodman, Ellen. "No change in political climate." *Boston Globe.* February 9, 2007. Accessed December 5, 2016. http://web.archive.org/web/20070214041353/http:/www.boston.

com/news/globe/editorial_opinion/oped/articles/2007/02/09/no_change_in_political_climate/.

26. Pomeroy, Ross. "Time to bring pseudoscience into science class!" *Real Clear Science.* April 03, 2014. Accessed December 5, 2016. http://www.realclearscience.com/blog/2014/04/its_time_to_teach_pseudoscience_in_science_class.html.

27. Popper, Karl R. 1963. "Science as falsification." 1963. Accessed March 29, 2017. http://www.stephenjaygould.org/ctrl/popper_falsification.html.

28. "The missing science from the draft national assessment on climate change." [undated]. Accessed March 29, 2017. https://object.cato.org/sites/cato.org/files/pubs/pdf/the-missing-science-of-draft-assessment.pdf.

29. "Debunking the irreducible complexity creationist argument against the scientific theory of evolution." February 5, 2014. Accessed March 29, 2017. http://exposingreligionblog.tumblr.com/post/75764067167.

30. Bart, January 8, 2016 (8:44 p.m.). Comment on Pierre Gosselin, "AGW theory is collapsed … Japanese scientist finds $CO_2$ climate sensitivity grandly overstated!," *No Tricks Zone*, January 08, 2016. Accessed December 5, 2016. http://notrickszone.com/2016/01/08/agw-theory-is-collapsed-japanese-scientist-finds-co2-climate-sensitivity-grandly-overstated-by-factor-of-three/#sthash.3gCo8RGM.oWrUOJLA.dpuf.

31. Hanson, Victor D. "Enemies of language," *The Washington Times*, November 23, 2016. Accessed December 6, 2016. http://www.washingtontimes.com/news/2016/nov/23/media-academia-enemies-of-language/.

32. "Randomness." [undated]. *Wikipedia*. Accessed December 6, 2016. https://en.wikipedia.org/wiki/Randomness.

33. "Randomness." [undated]. *The Free Dictionary by Farlex*. Accessed December 6, 2016.

34. http://www.thefreedictionary.com/randomness.

35. Eagle, Antony. "Chance versus randomness." First published Aug. 18, 2010; substantive revision Thu February 9, 2012. Accessed December 6, 2016. https://plato.stanford.edu/entries/chance-randomness/ *The Stanford Encyclopedia of Philosophy* (Winter 2016 Edition), Edward N. Zalta (ed.), https://plato.stanford.edu/archives/win2016/entries/chance-randomness/.

36. "Objections to evolution." *Wikipedia*. [undated]. Accessed December 6, 2016. https://en.wikipedia.org/wiki/Objections_to_evolution.

37. Barton, Nicholas H., et al. 2007. "Evidence for evolution." In: *Evolution*. Cold Springs Harbor, NY: Cold Spring Harbor Laboratory Press; 65, 83.

38. Key, Pam. "Richard Dawkins: 'Terrible indictment' of Ben Carson that he's 'ignorant' on evolution." *Breibart*, November 01, 2015. Accessed March 29, 2017. http://www.breitbart.com/video/2015/11/01/richard-dawkins-terrible-indictment-of-ben-carson-that-hes-ignorant-on-evolution/.

39. "Evolution deniers." *The Militant Atheist*. [undated]. Accessed December 6, 2016. http://the-militant-atheist.org/evolution-deniers.html.

40. "Fact." *Wikipedia*. [undated]. Accessed December 6, 2016. https://en.wikipedia.org/wiki/Fact.

41. "Objections to evolution." *Wikipedia*. [undated]. Accessed December 6, 2016. https://en.wikipedia.org/wiki/Objections_to_evolution.

42. Tomlinson, Hannah. Personal communication. "Circumstantial versus direct evidence." *Criminal Law Consulting For Writers & Filmmakers*. [undated]. Accessed December 6, 2016. http://www.criminallawconsulting.com/circumstantial-vs-direct-evidence.html.

43. "Evolution." 1993. In: *Merriam Webster's Collegiate Dictionary*. Springfield, MA, Merriam Webster, Inc., 10th ed., 402.

44. Wallace, Rick. "A case study bearing on the nature of 'consensus' in normal science and in the AGW controversy." *Watts Up With That?* March 10, 2016. Accessed December 6, 2016. https://wattsupwiththat.com/2016/03/10/a-case-study-bearing-on-the-nature-of-consensus-in-normal-science-and-in-the-agw-controversy/.

45. Nobel, D. "Claude Bernard, the first systems biologist, and the future of physiology." *Experimental. Physiology.* December 17, 2007. Accessed March 29, 2017. DOI: 10.1113/expphysiol.2007.038695.

46. Mayr, Ernst. 2001. "Appendix B." In: *What Evolution Is*. New York, NY: Basic Books, 276.

47. Barton, Nicholas H., et al. 2007. "Evidence for Evolution." In: *Evolution*. Cold Springs Harbor, NY: Cold Spring Harbor Laboratory Press, 65.

48. Barton, Nicholas H., et al. 2007. "Aim and Scope of the Book." In: *Evolution*. Cold Springs Harbor, NY: Cold Spring Harbor Laboratory Press, 2.

49. "Objections to evolution." *Wikipedia*. [undated]. Accessed December 6, 2016. https://en.wikipedia.org/wiki/Objections_to_evolution

50. Barton, Nicholas H., et al. 2007. "Evidence for Evolution." In: *Evolution*. Cold Springs Harbor, NY: Cold Spring Harbor Laboratory Press, 76.

51. Hendry, A.P., et al. "Evolutionary principles and their practical application." *Evolutionary Applications*. March 2011. Accessed March 29, 2017. DOI: 10.1111/j.1752-4571.2010.00165.x.

52. Holdrege, Craig. "The giraffe's short neck." *The Nature Institute*, Fall 2003. Accessed December 6, 2016. http://natureinstitute.org/pub/ic/ic10/giraffe.htm.

## CHAPTER 3

1. Heller, Tony. "Making Life From Scratch." *Real Science*. September 26, 2010. Accessed, December 7, 2016. http://stevengoddard.wordpress.com/2010/09/26/making-life-from-scratch/.

2. Barton, Nicholas H., et al. 2007. "LUCA and the Tree of Life." In: *Evolution*. Cold Springs Harbor, NY: Cold Spring Harbor Laboratory Press, 115.

3. "Cell structures and processes." [undated]. Accessed December 7, 2016. http://npc11bio.tripod.com/cells.htm.

4. Langer, A. "LANGER: Occam's Razor would cut regulation and boost the economy." *Washington Times*. July 31, 2013. December 7, 2016.

5. http://www.washingtontimes.com/news/2013/jul/31/occams-razor-would-cut-regulation-and-boost-the-ec/.

6. Metaxas, E. "Evolution Just Got Harder to Defend." *CNS News*. September 14, 2016. Accessed December 7, 2016. http://www.cnsnews.com/commentary/eric-metaxas/.

7.   Barton, Nicholas H., et al. 2007. "The origin of life." In: *Evolution*. Cold Springs Harbor, NY: Cold Spring Harbor Laboratory Press, 96–97.

8.   *U.S. National Library of Medicine National Institutes of Health; PubMed.* December 7, 2016.

9.   https://www.ncbi.nlm.nih.gov/pubmed/?term=DNA.

10.  Behe, Michael J. 1996. *Darwin's Black Box*, New York: Free Press.

11.  Luskin Casey. "Michael Behe's critics misunderstand irreducible complexity and make Darwinian evolution unfalsifiable." *Evolution News & Science Today.* March 10, 2011. Accessed December 7, 2016. http://www.evolutionnews.org/2011/03/michael_behes_critics_make_dar044511.html.

12.  Maimone, Tom. "Prebiotic Chemistry I." Mar. 2008. Accessed December 7, 2016. http://www.scripps.edu/baran/images/grpmtgpdf/Maimone_March_08.pdf.

13.  Barton, Nicholas H., et al. 2007. "The origin of life." In: *Evolution*. Cold Springs Harbor, NY: Cold Spring Harbor Laboratory Press, 93–95.

14.  Roston, Eric. "Scientists create tiniest life form yet, not sure what it is." *Bloomberg.* March 24, 2016. Accessed December 7, 2016. https://www.bloomberg.com/news/articles/2016-03-24/scientists-create-tiniest-life-form-yet-not-sure-what-it-is.

15.  Gauger, Ann. "Irreducible complex 'minimal' microbe evidence of intelligent design." *CNS News.* March 28, 2016. Accessed March 30, 2017. http://www.cnsnews.com/commentary/ann-gauger/irreducible-complex-minimal-microbe-evidence-intelligent-design.

## CHAPTER 4

1.   Hendry, A.P., et al. "Evolutionary principles and their practical application." *Evolutionary Applications.* March 2011. Accessed March 29, 2017. DOI: 10.1111/j.1752-4571.2010.00165.x.

2.   Nobel, D. "Claude Bernard, the first systems biologist, and the future of physiology." *Experimental Physiology.* December 18, 2007. Accessed December 8, 2016. DOI: 10.1113/expphysiol.2007.038695.

3.   "What is a genome?" *U. S. National Library of Medicine. Genetics Home Reference.* [undated]. Accessed December 8, 2016.  https://ghr.nlm.nih.gov/primer/hgp/genome.

4.   "What is a gene?" *U. S. National Library of Medicine. Genetics Home Reference.* [undated]. Accessed December 8, 2016. https://ghr.nlm.nih.gov/primer/basics/gene.

5.   Barton, Nicholas H., et al. 2007. "Selection on variation." In: *Evolution.* Cold Springs Harbor, NY: Cold Spring Harbor Laboratory Press, 463.

6.   Nobel, D. "Claude Bernard, the first systems biologist, and the future of physiology." *Experimental Physiology.* December 18, 2007. Accessed December 8, 2016. DOI: 10.1113/expphysiol.2007.038695.

7.   "What is a gene?" *U. S. National Library of Medicine. Genetics Home Reference.* [undated]. Accessed December 8, 2016. https://ghr.nlm.nih.gov/primer/basics/gene.

8.   "Haematopoesis." *Wikipedia.* [Undated.] Accessed December 8, 2016. https://en.wikipedia.org/wiki/Haematopoiesis.

9.   "What is a genome?" *U. S. National Library of Medicine. Genetics Home Reference.* [undated]. Accessed December 6, 2016. https://ghr.nlm.nih.gov/primer/hgp/genome.

10. Nobel, D. "Claude Bernard, the first systems biologist, and the future of physiology." *Experimental Physiology.* December 18, 2007. Accessed December 6, 2016. DOI: 10.1113/expphysiol.2007.038695.

11. "Breeds of Livestock." February 22, 1995. Department of Animal Science, Oklahoma State University. Accessed November 30, 2016. http://www.ansi.okstate.edu/breeds/.

12. The Editors at THF. 2011. "History of dog breeds." In: *The Encyclopedia of Dog Breeds.* Neptune City, NJ: THF Publications., Inc., 4.

13. The Editors at THF. 2011. [Cover] In: *The Encyclopedia of Dog Breeds.* Neptune City, NJ: THF Publications., Inc., 4.

14. Coile, D. Caroline. 2005. [Cover] In: *Encyclopedia of Dog Breeds.* Hauppauge, NY: Barron's Educational Series., VIII, Cover.

15. Coile, D. Caroline. 2005. "The toy group." In: *Encyclopedia of Dog Breeds.* Hauppauge, NY: Barron's Educational Series, 221.

16. Coile, D. Caroline. 2005. "The working group." In: *Encyclopedia of Dog Breeds.* Hauppauge, NY: Barron's Educational Series, 137.

17. "Pharaoh hound." *Dogtime.com.* [undated]. Accessed December 8, 2016. http://dogtime.com/dog-breeds/pharaoh-hound#/slide/1.

18. "Alaskan malamute." *Dogtime.com.* [undated]. Accessed December 8, 2016. http://dogtime.com/dog-breeds/alaskan-malamute.

19. Coile, D. Caroline. 2005. "The toy group." In: *Encyclopedia of Dog Breeds.* Hauppauge, NY: Barron's Educational Series, 221.

20. Coile, D. Caroline. 2005. "The working group." In: *Encyclopedia of Dog Breeds.* Hauppauge, NY: Barron's Educational Series, 127.

21. Carroll, Scott P., Trevor Fowles, and Crystal Perreira. "*Rhopalidae serinethinae* Soapberry Bugs of the world." Accessed December 8, 2016. http://www.soapberrybug.org/01_cms/details.asp?ID=5.

22. Barton, Nicholas H., et al. 2007. "Evidence for evolution." In: *Evolution.* Cold Springs Harbor, NY: Cold Spring Harbor Laboratory Press, 71–72.

23. Carroll, Scott P., Trevor Fowles, and Crystal Perreira. "*Rhopalidae serinethinae* Soapberry Bugs of the world." Accessed December 8, 2016. http://www.soapberrybug.org/01_cms/details.asp?ID=5.

24. Barton, Nicholas H., et al. 2007. "Evidence for evolution." In: *Evolution.* Cold Springs Harbor, NY: Cold Spring Harbor Laboratory Press, 71–72.

25. Dingle, H., S.P Carroll, and T.R. Famula. "Influence of genetic architecture on contemporary local evolution in the soapberry bug, *Jadera haematoloma*: artificial selection on beak length." *Journal of. Evolutionary Biology.* August 20, 2009. Accessed December 8, 2009. DOI: 10.1111/j.1420-9101.2009.01819.x.

## CHAPTER 5

1. "What was the biggest dinosaur? What was the smallest?" *United States Geologic Survey (USGS).* Accessed December 8, 2016. https://pubs.usgs.gov/gip/dinosaurs/sizes.html.

2. Nobel, D. "Claude Bernard, the first systems biologist, and the future of physiology." *Experimental Physiology.* December 18, 2007. Accessed December 6, 2016. DOI: 10.1113/expphysiol.2007.038695.

## CHAPTER 6

1.  Barton, Nicholas H., et al. 2007. "Evidence for evolution." In: *Evolution*. Cold Springs Harbor, NY: Cold Spring Harbor Laboratory Press, 76.

2.  Nobel, D. "Claude Bernard, the first systems biologist, and the future of physiology." *Experimental Physiology*. December 18, 2007. Accessed December 6, 2016. DOI: 10.1113/expphysiol.2007.038695.

3.  Barton, Nicholas H., et al. 2007. "Selection on variation." In: *Evolution*. Cold Springs Harbor, NY: Cold Spring Harbor Laboratory Press, 463.

4.  Barton, Nicholas H., et al. 2007. "Generation of variation by mutation and recombination." In: *Evolution*. Cold Springs Harbor, NY: Cold Spring Harbor Laboratory Press, 325.

5.  Barton, Nicholas H., et al. 2007. "Selection on variation." In: *Evolution*. Cold Springs Harbor, NY: Cold Spring Harbor Laboratory Press, 463.

## CHAPTER 7

1.  Lönnig, Wolf-Ekkehard. "The evolution of the long-necked giraffe (Part I)." October. 19, 2010. Accessed December 8, 2016. http://www.weloennig.de/Giraffe.pdf.

2.  Perkins, Sid. "Odd creature was ancient ancestor of to-day's giraffes." *Science*. November 24, 2015. Accessed December 8, 2016. http://www.sciencemag.org/news/2015/11/odd-creature-was-ancient-ancestor-today-s-giraffes.

3.  Strauss, Bob. [undated]. "10 Fun Facts About Giraffes." Accessed December 8, 2016. http://animals.about.com/od/animal-facts/ss/10-Fun-Facts-About-Giraffes.htm.

4.  Barton, Nicholas H., et al. 2007. "Selection on variation." In: *Evolution*. Cold Springs Harbor, NY: Cold Spring Harbor Laboratory Press, 463.

5.  "Giraffes in captivity." Accessed December 8, 2016. http://www. giraffeworlds.com/giraffes-in-captivity/.

6.  "Giraffe: Taxonomy: Evolution." *Wikipedia*. Accessed December 8, 2016. https://en.wikipedia.org/wiki/Giraffe#Evolution.

7.  Mitchell, G., J.D. Skinner. "An allometric analysis of the giraffe cardiovascular system." *Comparative Biochemistry and Physiology Part A: Molecular & Integrative Physiology*. December 2009. Accessed December 8, 2016. http://dx.doi.org/10.1016/j.cbpa.2009.08.013.

8.  American Heart Association. [undated]. "The Facts About High Blood Pressure." Accessed December 8, 2016. http:// www.heart.org/HEARTORG/Conditions/HighBloodPressure/ AboutHighBloodPressure/About-High-Blood-Pressure_ UCM_002050_Article.jsp#.

9.  Mayo Clinic. [undated]. "High blood pressure (hypertension). Blood pressure chart: what your reading means." Accessed December 8, 2016. http://www.mayoclinic.org/diseases-conditions/ high-blood-pressure/in-depth/blood-pressure/art-20050982.

10. The Centers for Disease Control and Prevention. [undated]. "Effects of High Blood Pressure." Accessed December 8, 2016. http://www. cdc.gov/bloodpressure/effects.htm.

11. Jacob, George. "Hypertension." [undated]. Accessed December 8, 2016. http://www.holistic-online.com/Remedies/heart/hypert_con- sequences.htm.

12. American Heart Association. "Understanding Blood Pressure Readings." [undated]. Accessed December 8, 2016. http://

www.heart.org/HEARTORG/Conditions/HighBloodPressure/AboutHighBloodPressure/Understanding-Blood-Pressure-Readings_UCM_301764_Article.jsp#.WEnEyWczU6Z.

13. Zhang, QG. "Hypertension and counter-hypertension mechanisms in giraffes." *Cardiovascular & Hematological Disorders - Drug Targets.* March 2006. Accessed December 8, 2016. http://www.ncbi.nlm.nih.gov/pubmed/16724937.

14. Mayo Clinic. "High blood pressure (hypertension). Blood pressure chart: what your reading means." [undated]. Accessed December 8, 2016. http://www.mayoclinic.org/diseases-conditions/high-blood-pressure/in-depth/blood-pressure/art-20050982.

15. "Circulatory system of the horse." *Wikipedia.* [undated]. Accessed December 8, 2016. https://en.wikipedia.org/wiki/Circulatory_system_of_the_horse.

16. "Blood Pressure Measurement." *Wikipedia.* [undated]. Accessed December 8, 2016. https://en.wikivet.net/Blood_Pressure_Measurement.

17. Zhang, QG. "Hypertension and counter-hypertension mechanisms in giraffes." *Cardiovascular & Hematological Disorders - Drug Targets.* March 2006. Accessed December 8, 2016. http://www.ncbi.nlm.nih.gov/pubmed/16724937.

18. Mitchell, G., J.D. Skinner. "An allometric analysis of the giraffe cardiovascular system." *Comparative Biochemistry and Physiology Part A: Molecular & Integrative Physiology.* December 2009. Accessed December 8, 2016. http://dx.doi.org/10.1016/j.cbpa.2009.08.013.

19. Giraffe Conservation Foundation. "Frequently asked questions about giraffe." [undated]. Accessed December 8, 2016. https://giraffeconservation.org/faqs/?v=7516fd43adaa.

20. Travel News Namibia. June 10, 2014. "Stick your neck out for giraffe conservation." June 21, 2014. World Giraffe Day. Accessed December 8, 2016. http://www.travelnewsnamibia.com/news/stick-neck-giraffe-conservation-jeans4giraffe/.

21. American Heart Association. [undated]. "Hypertensive Crisis: When You Should Call 9-1-1 for High Blood Pressure." Accessed December 8, 2016. http://www.heart.org/HEARTORG/Conditions/HighBloodPressure/AboutHighBloodPressure/Hypertensive-Crisis_UCM_301782_Article.jsp#.WEnJ8GczU6a.

22. Jacob, George. [undated]. "Hypertension." Accessed December 8, 2016. http://www.holistic-online.com/Remedies/heart/hypert_consequences.htm.

23. Binns, Corey. "Why giraffes don't get dizzy." June 26, 2006. Accessed December 8, 2016. http://www.livescience.com/853-giraffes-dizzy.html.

24. American Heart Association. [undated]. "How High Blood Pressure Can Lead to Kidney Damage or Failure." Accessed December 8, 2016. http://www.heart.org/HEARTORG/Conditions/HighBloodPressure/WhyBloodPressureMatters/Kidney-Damage-and-High-Blood-Pressure_UCM_301825_Article.jsp#.WEnNb2czU6Z.

25. Damkjaer, M, et al. "The giraffe kidney tolerates high arterial blood pressure by high renal interstitial pressure and low glomerular filtration rate." June 15, 2015. Accessed December 8, 2016. ACTA Physiologica. (Oxford) (Abstract; Conclusion) DOI: 10.1111/apha.12531.

26. Zhang, QG. "Hypertension and counter-hypertension mechanisms in giraffes." Cardiovascular & Hematological Disorders - Drug Targets. March 2006. Accessed December 8, 2016. http://www.ncbi.nlm.nih.gov/pubmed/16724937.

27. Strauss, Bob. [undated]. "10 Fun Facts About Giraffes." Accessed December 8, 2016. http://animals.about.com/od/animal-facts/ss/10-Fun-Facts-About-Giraffes.htm.

28. Petrillo, Brett. "Why Giraffes Don't Have Brain Damage." *BP's Fuel for Thought*. August 14, 2012. Accessed December 8, 2016. https://bpsfuelforthought.wordpress.com/2012/08/14/why-giraffes-dont-have-brain-damage/.

29. Lönnig WE. Oct. 19, 2010. The evolution of the long-necked giraffe (Part I). http://www.weloennig.de/Giraffe.pdf. Accessed December 8, 2016.

30. Akif'ev, AP. and GA Khudoliĭ. [Mutagenesis and genetic homeostasis in higher organisms]. *Vestn Ross Akad Med Nauk*. [Article in Russian] 1993. Accessed December 8, 2016. https://www.ncbi.nlm.nih.gov/pubmed/7682120.

31. Barton, Nicholas H., et al. 2007. "Selection on variation." In: *Evolution*. Cold Springs Harbor, NY: Cold Spring Harbor Laboratory Press, 463.

32. Akif'ev, AP. and GA Khudoliĭ. [Mutagenesis and genetic homeostasis in higher organisms]. *Vestn Ross Akad Med Nauk*. [Article in Russian] 1993. Accessed December 8, 2016. https://www.ncbi.nlm.nih.gov/pubmed/7682120.

33. Lönnig WE. Oct. 19, 2010. The evolution of the long-necked giraffe (Part I). http://www.weloennig.de/Giraffe.pdf. Accessed December 8, 2016.

34. Saylo, Monalie C., Cheryl C. Escoton, and Micah M. Saylo. "Punctuated equilibrium vs. phyletic gradualism." *International Journal of Bio-Science and Bio-Technology*. December 2011. Accessed March 29, 2017. http://www.sersc.org/journals/IJBSBT/vol3_no4/3.pdf.

Strobel, Lee. 2004. "The evidence of biological information: the challenge of DNA and the origin of life." In: *The Case for a Creator.* Grand Rapids, MI: Zondervan®; 298.

## CHAPTER 8

1.  "Lawsuit: CSUN Scientist fired after soft tissue found on dinosaur fossil." July 24, 2014. Accessed December 13, 2016.

2.  http://losangeles.cbslocal.com/2014/07/24/scientist-alleges-csun-fired-him-for-discovery-of-soft-tissue-on-dinosaur-fossil/.

3.  Turley, Jonathan. "Professor claims California state university fired him over his creationists belief." July 31, 2014. Accessed December 13, 2016.

4.  https://jonathanturley.org/2014/07/31/professor-claims-california-state-university-fired-him-over-his-creationists-belief/.

5.  Kabbany, Jennifer. "LAWSUIT: University fired scientist for finding soft tissue on dinosaur horn." *The College Fix.* July 25, 2014. Accessed December 13, 2016.

6.  http://www.thecollegefix.com/post/18549/.

7.  Haley, Garrett. "Dinosaur skin discovery threatens to debunk long-held evolutionary assumptions." *Christian News.* June 13, 2013. Accessed December 13, 2016.

8.  http://christiannews.net/2013/06/13/dinosaur-skin-discovery-threatens-to-debunk-long-held-evolutionary-assumptions/.

9.  Fields, Helen. "Dinosaur shocker." *Smithsonian.* May 2006. Accessed December 13, 2016. http://www.smithsonianmag.com/science-nature/dinosaur-shocker-115306469/?no-ist.

10. Barton, Nicholas H., et al. 2007. "Evidence for evolution." In: *Evolution.* Cold Springs Harbor, NY: Cold Spring Harbor Laboratory Press, 81.

11. Barton, Nicholas H., et al. 2007. "Evidence for evolution." In: *Evolution.* Cold Springs Harbor, NY: Cold Spring Harbor Laboratory Press, 81, 76.

## CHAPTER 9

1. Pearcey, Nancy. "Do biological facts no longer matter?" *CNS News.* May 20, 2016. Accessed December 12, 2016. http://www.cnsnews.com/commentary/nancy-pearcey/do-biological-facts-no-longer-matter.

2. "Secularism." [undated]. *New Advent Catholic Encyclopedia.* Accessed December 12, 2016. http://www.newadvent.org/cathen/13676a.htm.

3. Achenbach, Joel. "Carl Sagan denied being an atheist. So what did he believe?" [Part 1]. *Washington Post.* June 10, 2014. Accessed December 12, 2016. https://www.washingtonpost.com/news/achenblog/wp/2014/07/10/carl-sagan-denied-being-an-atheist-so-what-did-he-believe-part-1/?utm_term=.4c53834271b6.

4. Carl Sagan quotes. Accessed December 12, 2016. http://www.goodreads.com/quotes/178439-the-cosmos-is-all-that-is-or-was-or-ever.

5. Sproul, R.D., Keith Matheison, editors. 2005. *The Reformation Study Bible* (English Standard Version), 1848 (note to verse 8). Orlando, FL: Ligonier Ministries.

6. Barash, David P. "God, Darwin and my college biology class." *New York Times.* September 27, 2014. Accessed February 27, 2017. https://www.nytimes.com/2014/09/28/opinion/sunday/god-darwin-and-my-college-biology-class.html?_r=0.

7.  McElory, Molly. "David Barash explores science, religion and meaning of life in 'Buddhist Biology.'" *UW Today*. November 21, 2013. Accessed December 13, 2016.

8.  http://www.washington.edu/news/2013/11/21/david-barash-explores-science-religion-and-meaning-of-life-in-buddhist-biology/.

9.  Collins, Francis. 2006. *The Language of God*. New York, NY: Free Press.

10. Griffiths PE. "In What Sense Does 'Nothing Make Sense Except in the Light of Evolution'?" *Acta Biotheoretica*. http://link.springer.com/article/10.1007/s10441-008-9054-9.

11. Jones, Stephen E. "Dobzhansky was a religious man, although he . . . rejected . . . the existence of a personal God." *Creation Evolution Design*. September 9, 2006. Accessed December 13, 2016. http://creationevolutiondesign.blogspot.com/2006/09/dobzhansky-was-religious-man-although.html.

12. Spencer, Roy. "Climategate 2.0: Bias in scientific research." *Dr. Roy Spencer*. November 23, 2011. Accessed December 12, 2016. http://www.drroyspencer.com/2011/11/climategate-2-0-bias-in-scientific-research/.

13. Chambers, Oswald. 1994. *Daily Thoughts for Disciples*. Grand Rapids, MI: Discovery House. December 1 devotion.

14. "Dogma." *New Advent Catholic Encyclopedia.* [undated]. Accessed December 13, 2016. http://www.newadvent.org/cathen/05089a.htm.

15. American Association for the Advancement of Science. [Untitled letter to OK Sen. Straton Taylor] March 20, 2006. Accessed December 5, 2016.

16. http://www.aaas.org/sites/default/files/migrate/uploads/0322ok.pdf.

17. BrainyQuote: Richard Dawkins "Faith is the great cop-out . . ." [undated]. Accessed December 14, 2016. https://www.brainyquote.com/quotes/quotes/r/richarddaw141335.html.

18. "Using some common terms carefully and accurately in scientific speech and writing." [undated]. Accessed December 14, 2016. http://oregonstate.edu/instruction/bb317/scientifictheories.html.

19. "NABT position statement on teaching evolution." *National Association of Biology Teachers.* 2011. Accessed December 14, 2016. http://www.nabt.org/websites/institution/?p=92.

20. Forrest, Barbara. "Understanding the intelligent design creationist movement: its true nature and goals. A position paper from the center for inquiry office of public policy." 2007. Accessed December 14, 2016. http://www.centerforinquiry.net/uploads/attachments/intelligent-design.pdf.

21. Lopez, Steve. "Does creationism have a place at a public school?" *Los Angeles Times.* December 08, 2012. Accessed December 14, 2016. http://articles.latimes.com/2012/dec/08/local/la-me-1209-lopez-christian-20121207.

22. Dolak, Kevin. (via Good Morning America). "Bill Nye 'The science guy' hits evolution deniers." *ABC News.* August 27, 2012. Accessed December 14, 2016. http://abcnews.go.com/blogs/technology/2012/08/bill-nye-the-science-guy-hits-evolution-deniers/.

23. Nye, Bill. 2015. "Me You and Evolution, Too." In: *Undeniable*, ed. Corey S. Powell. New York, NY: St. Martin's Griffen, 4.

24. Hall, Wynton. "White House petition to ban creationism gathering steam." *Breitbart.* June 21, 2013. Accessed December 14, 2016. http://www.breitbart.com/big-government/2013/06/21/white-house-petition-to-ban-creationism-gathering-steam/.

25. Ming-Jin Liu, Cai-Hua Xiong, Le Xiong, Xiao-Lin Huang. Biomechanical Characteristics of Hand Coordination in Grasping Activities of Daily Living. *PLoS ONE*. January 5, 2016. Accessed December 14, 2016. http://journals.plos.org/plosone/article?id=10.1371/journal.pone.0146193.

26. Klinghoffer, David. "Mob with pitchforks forms as science journal *PLOS ONE* acknowledges 'proper design by the creator.'" *Evolution News*. March 3, 2016. Accessed December 14, 2016. http://www.evolutionnews.org/2016/03/mob_with_pitchf102658.html.

27. Metaxas, Eric. "Scientism out of hand: 'Creatorgate' and the sorry state of science." *CNS News*. April 5, 2016. Accessed December 14, 2016. http://www.cnsnews.com/commentary/eric-metaxas/.

28. DeYoung, Don. 2005. "Radioisotope dating case studies." In: *Thousands, Not Billions*. Master Books; 138, 174, 176.

29. Kabbany, Jennifer. "Lawsuit: University fired scientist for finding soft tissue on dinosaur horn." *The College Fix*. Jul. 25, 2014. Accessed December 13, 2016. http://www.thecollegefix.com/post/18549/.

30. Turley, Jonathan. "Professor claims California state university fired him over his creationists belief." *Jonathan Turley*. July 31, 2014. Accessed December 13, 2016.

31. https://jonathanturley.org/2014/07/31/professor-claims-california-state-university-fired-him-over-his-creationists-belief/.

32. "Lawsuit: CSUN Scientist fired after soft tissue found on dinosaur fossil." *CBS Los Angeles*. July 24, 2014. Accessed December 13, 2016. http://losangeles.cbslocal.com/2014/07/24/scientist-alleges-csun-fired-him-for-discovery-of-soft-tissue-on-dinosaur-fossil/.

33. Chambers, Oswald. 1963. *My Utmost for His Highest*. Uhrichsville, OH: Barbour Publishing. July 18 devotion.

34. Weikart, Richard. "Are humans worthy of greater dignity and protection than animals?" *CNS News*. April 8, 2016. Accessed December 13, 2016. http://www.cnsnews.com/commentary/richard-weikart/are-humans-qualitatively-distinct-animals-worthy-greater-dignity-and.

35. Klinghoffer, David. "'Undeniable': Darwinian explanations not just unlikely, but 'physically impossible.'" *CNS News*. July 13, 2016. Accessed December 13, 2016. http://www.cnsnews.com/commentary/david-klinghoffer/undeniable-darwinian-explanations-are-not-just-unlikely-physically.

## CHAPTER 10

1. Heller, Tony. "Einstein said that all serious scientists believe in intelligent design." *Real Science*. November 9, 2013. Accessed December 13, 2016. https://stevengoddard.wordpress.com/2013/11/09/einstein-said-that-all-serious-scientists-believe-in-intelligent-design/.

2. Colson, Chuck. "Christians – not the enlightenment – invented modern science." *CNS News*. October 10, 2016. Accessed December 13, 2016. http://www.cnsnews.com/commentary/chuck-colson/weve-been-lied-christians-not-enlightenment-invented-modern-science.

## APPENDIX I

1. Brainy Quote. [undated]. Richard P. Feynman Quote: "The first principle . . . " Accessed December 13. 2016. https://www.brainyquote.com/quotes/quotes/r/richardpf137642.html.

2. Franklin, Corey. "The silencing of global warming critics." *Chicago Tribune*. May 21, 2014. Accessed December 13, 2016. http://www.chicagotribune.com/news/opinion/commentary/ct-perspec-climate-0521-20140521,0,1067988.story.

3.  Watts, Anthony. "Consensus climate science: What would Thomas Huxley say?" *Watts up With That?* April 16, 2009. Accessed December 14, 2016. https://wattsupwiththat.com/2009/04/16/consensus-climate-science-what-would-thomas-huxley-say/.

4.  BrainyQuote: Albert Einstein. "No amount of experimentation . . . " [undated]. Accessed December 14, 2016. https://www.brainyquote.com/quotes/quotes/a/alberteins100017.html.

5.  Franklin, Corey. "The silencing of global warming critics." *Chicago Tribune.* May 21, 2014. Accessed December 4, 2016. http://articles.chicagotribune.com/2014-05-21/opinion/ct-perspec-climate-0521-20140521_1_climate-scientists-climate-change-climate-debate.

6.  Morrissey, Ed. "Make the Pill an over-the-counter medication." *Hot Air.* December 14, 2012. Accessed December 14, 2016. http://hotair.com/archives/2012/12/14/jindal-make-the-pill-an-over-the-counter-medication/.

7.  Goodreads: Carl Sagan. "Science is more than a body of knowledge . . . " [undated]. http://www.goodreads.com/quotes/962093-science-is-more-than-a-body-of-knowledge-it-is.

8.  Chambers, Oswald. 1994. *Daily Thoughts for Disciples.* Grand Rapids, MI: Discovery House. December 11 devotion.

9.  "Glossary of common site terms." *U.S. National Institutes of Health; ClinicalTrials.* [undated]. Accessed December 14, 2016. https://clinicaltrials.gov/ct2/about-studies/glossary#D.

10. "Glossary of common site terms." *U.S. National Institutes of Health; ClinicalTrials.* [undated]. Accessed December 14, 2016. https://clinicaltrials.gov/ct2/about-studies/glossary#D.

11.  "Double Dummy Technique." *On Biostatistics and Clinical Trials.* June 12, 2009. Accessed December 14, 2016. http://onbiostatistics.blogspot. com/2009/06/double-dummy-technique.html.

12.  Collins, Francis. 2006. *The Language of God.* New York, NY: Free Press, 112–115.

13.  Watts, Anthony. "The Higgs boson takes science center stage for 2012." *Watts Up With That?* December 23, 2012. Accessed December 14, 2016. https://wattsupwiththat.com/2012/12/23/ the-higgs-boson-takes-science-center-stage-for-2012/.

14.  Large Hadron Collider. *Wikipedia.* [undated]. Accessed December 14, 2016. https://en.wikipedia.org/wiki/Large_Hadron_Collider.

15.  CERN. "The Higgs boson." [undated]. Accessed December 14, 2016. http://home.cern/topics/higgs-boson.

16.  Hulme, Mike. "The appliance of science." *The Guardian.* March 13, 2007. Accessed December 14, 2016. https://www.theguardian. com/society/2007/mar/14/scienceofclimatechange.climatechange.

17.  Heller, Tony. "Eisenhower's prophetic warning from 55 years ago." *Real Science.* February 4, 2015. Accessed December 14, 2016. https://stevengoddard.wordpress.com/2015/02/04/ eisenhowers-prophetic-warning-from-55-years-ago/.

18.  "Post-normal science." *Wikipedia.* [undated]. Accessed December 14, 2016. https://en.wikipedia.org/wiki/Post-normal_science.

19.  Beisner, E. Calvin. "Science publisher calls for better communications – but not of science." *Watts Up With That?* October 20, 2012. Accessed December 14, 2016. https://wattsupwiththat. com/2012/10/20/science-publisher-calls-for-better-communications-but-not-of-science/.

20. Johnson, Phillip E. 2010. "Darwinist religion." In: *Darwin on Trial*. Downers Grove: InterVarsity Press.

21. Hughes, Austin L. "The folly of scientism." *The New Atlantis*. Fall 2002. Accessed March 31, 2016. http://www.thenewatlantis.com/publications/the-folly-of-scientism.

22. Metaxas, Eric. "Scientism out of hand: 'Creatorgate' and the sorry state of science." *CNS News*. April 5, 2016. Accessed December 14, 2016. http://www.cnsnews.com/commentary/eric-metaxas/.

23. "The Law of Mass Action." The Free Dictionary. [undated]. Accessed December 14, 2016. http://www.thefreedictionary.com/law+of+mass+action.

24. "Fick's laws of diffusion." Wikipedia. [undated]. Accessed December 14, 2016. https://en.wikipedia.org/wiki/Fick's_laws_of_diffusion.

25. "Antimetabolites." *Drugs.com*. [undated]. Accessed December 14, 2016. https://www.drugs.com/drug-class/antimetabolites.html.

26. "Fluorouracil: fluorouracil injection, solution." *U.S. National Library of Medicine. Daily Med*. [undated]. Accessed December 14, 2016. https://dailymed.nlm.nih.gov/dailymed/drugInfo.cfm?setid=8eff167f-203a-4a81-b2fc-d8773bc3555e.

27. "Cytarabine- cytarabine injection." *U.S. National Library of Medicine. Daily Med*. [undated]. Accessed December 14, 2016. https://dailymed.nlm.nih.gov/dailymed/drugInfo.cfm?setid=b48842dd-c5c9-484c-a3f5-cb883919b418.

## GLOSSARY

1. Tomlinson H. Personal communication.

2.  "Circumstantial versus direct evidence." *Criminal Law Consulting For Writers & Filmmakers.* [undated]. Accessed December 14, 2016. http://www.criminallawconsulting.com/circumstantial-vs-direct-evidence.html.

3.  "Empirical evidence." *Wikipedia.* [undated]. Accessed December 14, 2016. https://en.wikipedia.org/wiki/Empirical_evidence.

4.  "Empirical." 1993. In: *Merriam Webster's Collegiate Dictionary.* Springfield, MA, Merriam Webster, Inc., 10th ed., 379.

5.  "What is a genome?" *U. S. National Library of Medicine. Genetics Home Reference.* [undated]. Accessed December 8, 2016. https://ghr.nlm.nih.gov/primer/hgp/genome.

6.  "What is a gene?" *U. S. National Library of Medicine. Genetics Home Reference.* [undated]. Accessed December 8, 2016. https://ghr.nlm.nih.gov/primer/basics/gene.

7.  Nobel, D. "Claude Bernard, the first systems biologist, and the future of physiology." *Experimental. Physiology.* December 17, 2007. Accessed March 29, 2017. DOI: 10.1113/expphysiol.2007.038695.

8.  "Inference." *Merriam Webster.* [undated]. Accessed December 14, 2016. https://www.merriam-webster.com/dictionary/inference.

9.  "Abductive reasoning." [undated]. Accessed December 14, 2016. http://www.newworldencyclopedia.org/entry/Abductive_reasoning.

10. "What is a gene mutation and how do mutations occur?" *U. S. National Library of Medicine. Genetics Home Reference.* [undated]. Accessed December 14, 2016. https://ghr.nlm.nih.gov/primer/mutationsanddisorders/genemutation.

11. "Sequela" *MedicineNet.com.* [undated]. Accessed December 14, 2016. http://www.medicinenet.com/script/main/art.asp?articlekey=23895.

For more information about
## H. Robert Wilson, Ph.D.
&
## *Nullifying God: Evolution's End Game*
## *A Scientist's Challenge*

please visit:

*wilsonevolution7@gmail.com*
*@NullifyingGod*
*www.facebook.com/NullifyingGod*


For more information about
AMBASSADOR INTERNATIONAL
please visit:

*www.ambassador-international.com*
*@AmbassadorIntl*
*www.facebook.com/AmbassadorIntl*

# ABOUT THE AUTHOR

 Dr. Wilson is a retired research biologist and holds a PhD in Zoology with training in anatomy, physiology, and pathology. He spent much of his 33-year career in the pharmaceutical industry evaluating new drugs for certain infectious diseases and cancer. Bob has been married since 1964 to his beautiful wife, Lynn, and the couple has two children and four grandchildren. He has been a Christian for more than 40 years and has served as a Bible study leader as well as a group leader in a Teen Community Bible Study. Bob and Lynn live in Beaufort, NC.